LESSONS FROM THE DEPRESSION

Eliminating Debt the Old-Fashioned Way

By

Darlene Gudrie Butts

iUniverse, Inc.
New York   Bloomington

Lessons from the Depression
Eliminating Debt the Old-Fashioned Way

Copyright © 2009, Darlene Gudrie Butts

All rights reserved. No part of this book may be used or reproduced by any means, graphic, electronic, or mechanical, including photocopying, recording, taping or by any information storage retrieval system without the written permission of the publisher except in the case of brief quotations embodied in critical articles and reviews.

The information, ideas, and suggestions in this book are not intended to render professional advice. Before following any suggestions contained in this book, you should consult your personal accountant or other financial advisor. Neither the author nor the publisher shall be liable or responsible for any loss or damage allegedly arising as a consequence of your use or application of any information or suggestions in this book.

iUniverse books may be ordered through booksellers or by contacting:

iUniverse
1663 Liberty Drive
Bloomington, IN 47403
www.iuniverse.com
1-800-Authors (1-800-288-4677)

Because of the dynamic nature of the Internet, any Web addresses or links contained in this book may have changed since publication and may no longer be valid. The views expressed in this work are solely those of the author and do not necessarily reflect the views of the publisher, and the publisher hereby disclaims any responsibility for them.

ISBN: 978-1-4401-3580-4 (sc)
ISBN: 978-1-4401-3581-1 (e-book)

Library of Congress Control Number: 2009926417

Printed in the United States of America

iUniverse rev. date: 4/15/2009

Disclaimer

The information, ideas, and suggestions in this book are not intended to render professional advice. Before following any suggestions contained in this book, you should consult your personal accountant or other financial advisor. Neither the author nor the publisher shall be liable or responsible for any loss or damage allegedly arising as a consequence of your use or application of any information or suggestions in this book. We assume no responsibility for errors, inaccuracies, omissions, or any inconsistencies herein.

All the characters in this book are fictitious. Any resemblance to actual persons, living or dead, is purely coincidental.

To Ron

Twenty-six years ago, you started on a journey with me with the vow, "for richer or poorer." Thank you for never giving up on me.

Contents

Acknowledgments	xi
Note from the Author	xiii
Chapter 1 – Declined	1
Chapter 2—How Bad Is It?	7
Chapter 3 – The Truth Shall Set You Free	12
Chapter 4 – There Is No Easy Way Out	17
Chapter 5 – Cutting Expenses	22
Chapter 6 – Beating Credit Card Bullies	31
Chapter 7 – Keep Asking until They Reduce Your Rate	36
Chapter 8 – Having Fun for Free	42
Chapter 9 – Celebrate the Baby Steps	48
Chapter 10 – Boosting Income to Balance the Budget	56
Chapter 11 – Make Money Doing What You Love	62
Chapter 12 – Once You Commit to Change, Change Will Happen	68
Chapter 13 – Breaking Old Habits	72
Chapter 14 – Ask for Help	77
Chapter 15 – Have Faith	86
Chapter 16 – Everyone Needs an Emergency Fund	91
Chapter 17 - Benefits of Giving	96
Chapter 18 – If at First You Don't Succeed, Try Again	102
Chapter 19 – Savings versus Debt Reduction	111
Chapter 20 – Making an Automatic Plan	119
Chapter 21 – Having a Positive Attitude	126
Chapter 22 – The Journey Is More Important than the Destination	133

Chapter 23 – Investments 101   143

Chapter 24 – Sometimes Old-Fashioned Is Best   152

Acknowledgments

Coming up with the idea for this book and then writing it and publishing it was no easy task. It was even more difficult because it is my first book. There were many people who helped along the way.

I first want to thank those clients who gave me the idea of writing a simple book about dealing with debt. It is their idea and I hope I did it justice.

I would like to thank each of my mentors who made me believe that I could do it. It started with the movie *The Secret*. From there, I have learned so much from Mike Dooley, Neale Donald Walsch, Peggy McColl, Bob Proctor, Jack Canfield, and Mark Victor Hanson. I have not met any of them personally, but their conference calls, e-mails, and books gave me all the personal tools I needed to follow my dreams. I also want to thank Heather Picken, who helped me break free of my own barriers.

I would like to thank Chris Guerriero at Automatic Best Seller for the information to get started. Thanks also to everyone at iUniverse who made it happen.

My sister Joanne was the first to read this book; she helped me with the first series of edits and revisions. Thanks, Jo, for the encouragement.

David Chilton is my inspiration, and he generously gave advice, especially about self-publishing.

My undying gratitude and love goes to my entire family and my friends who cheered me on and listened to me ramble longer than

I should have about this project. I especially have to thank my inner circle, Ron, Nick, Kalina, and Livi, who paid the dearest price but remained my strongest supporters.

Finally, I want to thank God. This is his work.

The information in this book comes from my experiences. It is now passed on to you to make your path easier on the road to financial security. Enjoy!

Note from the Author

I have enjoyed a career for the past twenty-two years as a certified financial adviser. Currently, I am living near the "car capital" of Canada; we have endured bad news for more than two years now. Plants are closing and spin-off jobs are disappearing. The real estate prices have been dropping for more than eighteen months. My husband and I are in the two areas of the economy that you do not want to be in right now: automotive and financial.

A year ago, I had several clients ask me to help them deal with their debt problems. I had recommended different books to them, but each came back asking for a simpler guide. They did not want to look at charts or statistics. They wanted me to tell them how others were coping. That is when I came up with the idea of telling a parable that had all the steps woven in. It is easier to learn through a story than through graphs and pie charts. I also wanted to deal with the emotional side of being in debt.

I believe that being in debt is a symptom, not the problem. It is very much like being overweight. If you just diet and don't take care of the underlying problem, you will gain the weight back. Debt works the same way; if you don't look at why you got into financial trouble, you will struggle with this throughout the rest of your life. We tend to compensate for unhappiness by buying things. I know of many instances where consolidation loans were used, and a year later, the credit cards were run up again. There are many people who have claimed bankruptcy more than once. You need to deal with the underlying problems of your whole life, as well as your financial problems, to finally be financially free.

Interestingly enough, as I began to write this book, my own financial situation began to deteriorate. This personal crisis has been a blessing because this book now has an authenticity and an emotional depth that would not have been achieved otherwise. I have literally been there. I also had to look at my life and determine why this was happening. How could a professional get into this much trouble? I learned that there were things I needed to change in my life that had nothing to do with money. By using the same steps outlined in this book, I have been able to find success during a year that has challenged me financially and emotionally.

I hope by reading this story, you will not feel alone. Millions of people are living this same story. But that story can change. All you need is the strength and courage to make it happen. You may find, as Tim and Tricia did in the story, that your whole life will change for the better.

All the best,

Darlene Gudrie Butts

Chapter 1 – Declined

"Declined," said the cashier.

"That can't be right. Try it again," said Tricia.

The girl rolled her eyes and swiped the card again. "Declined," she said in a louder voice.

Tricia cringed. "I am telling you, that can't be right. Do it again."

"Ma'am, if I run your card again and it says declined, they will ask me to take it away from you. Do you want that?"

Tricia hesitated for a moment, grabbed her card, and then started to walk away. She mumbled over her shoulder, "By the way, I am not a *ma'am*. I am only twenty-nine years old."

The stares of the other customers burned into her back as she exited the store. What the hell was going on? She was sure that she had at least $200 left on that card. That thought kept repeating in her head as she got into her car. *I should have $200 left.* She starting punching the steering wheel, repeating aloud, "I should have $200 left." Then she began to sob.

Tricia felt as if she had hit rock bottom. She had been creatively keeping their finances afloat, and now it was over. Tears of humiliation ran down her face. She wondered how she could go home now, without the groceries. How was she going to explain? What were they going to do?

As she drove home, she tried to think back to what went wrong. Four years ago, she and her husband Tim moved into a cute bungalow on Parkside with their two children. Her family was very happy. All she could remember was laughter. It was so simple. Not anymore.

While living in that little house, she dreamed of living in Waverly, a small neighborhood in Stanton that had Victorian houses with wrap-around porches and huge backyards. Eventually, she made an appointment with a mortgage broker, without even telling Tim. She wanted to know what she had to do to own one of those houses. The broker told her that they couldn't afford to live there yet. All she had to do was save some more money for the down payment and come back.

Tricia was never good at hearing the word *no*. She found out what she needed to have, and she decided she would make it appear like they had it on paper. It wasn't easy deceiving a professional. She spent hours moving a little money here and shuffling a little there until she had found a mortgage broker who said yes.

She would never forget the day she told Tim. He didn't understand why she wanted to move. They had it made, he said. But the more Tricia thought about it, the more she knew she wouldn't be happy again until they moved to Waverly. It took several months to find the perfect house. She was sure that their house would sell in a few days because all the homes for sale in her area had sold quickly. They put in an unconditional offer to get the best bang for their buck and did a ninety-day closing to give them plenty of time to sell. Tricia felt that she had done well.

Two days after they signed the deal, the Fairfax cardboard factory caught on fire. It was the largest employer in Stanton, and now half the town was on layoff. The world just stopped. They had fewer than ninety days to sell their house in a market that had come to a standstill, and Tim's job was on hold. Tricia was bitter. She had worked hard to come up with a creative scheme to get her dream home, and now this. Why couldn't she catch a break? She was miserable.

She felt like her life had been one misfortune after another. She never had a close relationship with her mother; shopping was the only activity they could do together without fighting. Her father worked long hours, and she did not get to see much of him when she was growing up. She got pregnant in her first year of college, so she had to quit and marry Tim before the birth. The day after her son's birth, her father passed away unexpectedly. She spent months going between the unbelievable happiness she felt when she looked at her son Kyle to the raw grief she felt when thinking about his namesake, her father.

She looked at her present life as a continuation of the past. She moped around the house and felt sorry for herself. There were days when she could not even get out of bed, let alone get dressed. The emotional burden of this crisis was too heavy to bear. Tim had no idea how bad it was, and Tricia did not want him to know. So when he asked her what was wrong, she told him she just wasn't feeling well. There was no reason to bring him down as well.

She started to miss work, which only compounded the problem. She went to her doctor with various complaints. He prescribed something for her, but she knew in her heart that pills were not the answer. The doctor could not fix what she had done. He could not make her better.

It took weeks for her instinct to fight to return. Tricia wasn't sure what the turning point was. She just knew that she couldn't wait around for the horrible ending any longer and she needed to do something to try to stop it. She had always been able to work her way out of a jam before, and she would handle this one as well. So she became an expert in marketing a home.

She learned about staging a house and she also lowered the price to reflect the new market. She made sure there were cookies and punch for every open house and the place was spotless. She read books on selling real estate and lived for the TV show *Please Sell* that came on every night at seven. As long as they sold before closing on their new home, they would survive.

The days passed and they had a conditional offer, but their home had not officially sold yet. Tricia began to panic. This was the day they took possession of their house in Waverly; they would now have double payments. The clock was no longer ticking until closing day. It was now clicking down to the day she would not have any money.

Tricia did not want anyone to know that she was in trouble. She had told Tim that they were just fine, and she needed him to keep on believing that. She kept life as normal as possible. The household budget remained the same, with a trip to McDonald's once a week for the kids and Jack's Pub every Friday night for Tim and Tricia. Her housekeeper was a godsend as she tried to juggle two kids, two homes, and a part-time job. She knew this was only temporary, so she borrowed from her credit cards as a short-term solution. When the house finally sold, they would have more than enough to pay everything back, and life would be as it was.

Six months later, they finally received some good news. Someone was presenting a cash offer. The real estate broker didn't say the dollar value of the offer, but they were looking forward to making the deal work. Tricia would never forget the feeling in her stomach when she saw the number. It was $20,000 below their asking price and left nothing extra to pay off the new debt. In fact, after closing costs, they would probably owe money. But if they didn't accept the offer, the monthly payments on both houses would far outweigh their income. They would continue to get further behind. This devastated Tricia.

Within a month of closing the deal, Tricia realized they were in bigger trouble than she had thought. In those six months, three out of the four credit cards reached their limits. Adding those payments to the increased mortgage payment of the new house, she was still falling behind. Tim was back to work, but there was no overtime because the plant was still on reduced production. It was his overtime income that paid for all the luxuries. She needed that income to keep their heads above water. She decided to go back to the mortgage broker and see about refinancing.

The broker was abrupt with her; Tricia wasn't sure whether it was because he had caught on to her deception or he felt frustrated about not being able to help her. With falling real estate prices, the credit card debt, and Tim's lower income, there would be no institution that would lend them money.

Unfortunately for Tricia, they did not have parents who could help them out. She wasn't even sure where her mother was living. She had left town with her father's best friend six months after the funeral, and Tricia hadn't spoken to her since. Tim's parents had spent the last five years traveling the world and taking jobs along the way to help pay for it. They both believed they were still eighteen. The only money they had was what they were using to live on.

Tricia didn't have many friends, and even if she did, she would be too humiliated to ask for money. The only person left was her Crazy Grammy Ti. Crazy Grammy Ti had always terrified Tricia. She seemed angry and mean, and they only visited her once a year on Christmas Eve. She hadn't seen her since her father passed away. Thinking back, she couldn't believe that it had been that long. She would never be able to approach her for money.

The day at the grocery store was the lowest point in Tricia's life. She could no longer pretend that everything was normal. The problem had gotten too big and she had no real solution. She was just so tired. She wanted all the lies and phone calls to stop. The credit card companies were starting to call daily, and she no longer had any money to move from one card to pay another. The money game was over and she felt like her life was over as well. She had hoped every day for the last year that it was all going to work out, but it hadn't. Fear and humiliation paralyzed her. She just wanted it all to go away.

When the realization came that she might lose her home, Tricia thought again about her grandmother. She was desperate. She was just so tired of feeling overwhelmed and full of fear. Every night before she fell asleep, she had waves of panic wash over her. She had trouble functioning during the day because she was so worried. Tricia decided that calling her grandmother couldn't be any worse than losing their house. She was nervous dialing and almost hung up. Her grandmother was curt on the phone but agreed that Tricia could come over on Saturday afternoon.

The next three days were nerve-wracking for her as she played the upcoming meeting over and over in her mind. What she imagined was not pleasant. She didn't know how she was going to ask her estranged grandmother to help her out of this disaster. She wanted a solution badly, but her grandmother scared her. In this emotional turmoil, she both dreaded and longed for the meeting on Saturday.

Lesson from Chapter 1

People Make Mistakes

You are not the first or the last person to make a mistake big enough to put your financial future in jeopardy. We are human and we are here to learn lessons. It may not seem fair and it may be painful, but why would we be here unless it is to learn?

Your first step is to forgive yourself. You cannot move forward until you have accepted responsibility for where you are and forgiven your own mistakes. This can be a difficult step.

Your second step is to forgive anyone else who was part of the problem. You delay a solution when you hang on to blame. No one can change the actions of their past. When you stop blaming yourself and others, change will begin.

The last step is to reach out to someone for help. Many people will help if given the opportunity. Just start asking. Again, this is a difficult step. Shame keeps us from sharing our story. We do not want anyone to know that we have failed. There is no shame in taking control of your life and fixing your mistakes.

Chapter 2—How Bad Is It?

When she walked into her father's boyhood home, the musty smell brought back memories of earlier visits. She remembered asking her father why old people's homes smelled funny. He said, "Because everything was old in the house and you could smell the past in them."

She sat on the edge of the couch until her grandmother broke the silence. "Well, what do you want?"

Tricia was a little shocked and then angered by this rude start to her visit. Why did she have to act like this? Over the past three days, Tricia had thought about what to say and decided instead of skirting the issue she would get right to it. "I'm in trouble," she said.

"What kind of trouble?" her grandmother asked.

"Money trouble," said Tricia.

"Ah." After an awkward silence, her grandmother continued, "So you want to borrow money, do you? That's what you came for?"

"Yes, I need to borrow money."

"Well, I'm not going to lend you any."

That was Tricia's worst fear. She counted on this money, and her grandmother said no. Now what was she going to do? She got up to leave, but her grandmother interrupted.

"But I will help you."

"How can you help without a loan?" Tricia asked.

"I will teach you how to get out of your trouble. I have some experience in that area," she said softly.

Tricia sank back into the couch. She *was* going to help her. But how could she help her without lending her money? Tricia had thought everything through and decided that borrowing money was the only solution. She needed money and she needed it fast.

"Why can't you just lend me the money?" Tricia asked in defeat.

"If I lend money to you, you won't learn anything and you will be back in three months wanting more. I am not a bank."

"I promise you, I won't be back," Tricia said defiantly.

"Yes you will. I know all about it. Been through it with your dad, and I learned my lesson. Your mom always had big dreams; wanting everything and living high. Your dad spent most of his life trying to figure out how to pay for it. That is why you stopped coming regularly. Your father had a hard time facing me knowing how much he owed me. I won't let that happen again."

This news shocked Tricia. She had spent her childhood thinking she could have whatever she wanted and never worried about money. Once in a while, she would hear a snippet of conversation between her parents about spending and paying. She never really paid much attention. As far as she knew, she grew up in a household with sound finances, and her father took care of everything. She would have never guessed he had borrowed money from his mother.

Tricia sank into the couch. Emotions swirled around her. She felt as if someone had just punched her in the stomach; she was having problems breathing. She had no other choice but to listen to her grandmother. She had run out of options.

"What am I supposed to do?" asked Tricia.

"First, I need to know where you are now. How bad is it? Do you even know?"

"I can't tell you exact numbers, but I know it is bad. We don't have enough coming in to cover everything going out. The credit card companies are calling day and night. They are threatening to padlock my house and have Tim's wages garnished. One guy said he would come to the house to get money if I didn't pay them. I am getting scared. I can't pay anyone right now." Tricia started sobbing. She hadn't realized how panicked she was and now, without money from her grandmother, she didn't know what to do.

"We will talk more about how to deal with the credit card

companies later, but you need to know there are some basic rules. They can't come to your house. In fact, if someone threatens you again, report them. That is illegal. Foreclosure and garnishing of wages is a long process through the courts. If you haven't received a letter stating that this has begun, we still have time. You need to know the mortgage, heat, water, and food come first. You must make sure you cover your family's basic needs before sending any more money out. I can help you with that. We will work this out."

As Tricia's sobs subsided, Ti wasn't sure whether she should go over and comfort her granddaughter or not. It was awkward because it had been so long since she had seen her. They were almost strangers. Ti stayed where she was.

"You will come back Saturday with a list of all of your assets and all of your debts. I also need a list of every payment you have to make and every expense you have, big or small. I want to see where you have spent your money for the last two months. It will surprise you how much money is going out for nothing. Last but not least, you need to bring Tim. Then we can start getting this fixed."

Tricia jumped up. "Tim! Why do you need Tim here? I don't want him to know. Either you help me in secret or I will do it on my own."

"Well, doing it on your own hasn't worked. You shouldn't keep secrets in a marriage. Look what happened to your parents. If you are going to get out of this mess, it will take the pair of you to do it. The kids need to be here as well. They should know what is going on. I want the whole family here. Take it or leave it."

Her grandmother was glaring at her, and Tricia knew there was no arguing. How was she going to tell Tim? He would leave her. She was ashamed and humiliated. She failed to take care of her family and she deserved to lose them. Her grandmother needed to know why she couldn't tell him.

"You know he will leave me," Tricia sighed.

"No he won't. It took both of you to get into this mess and it will take both of you to get out of it. You have been keeping this burden to yourself for too long. You need him, Patricia. You cannot do this alone anymore. Your father died of the stress of trying to do it on his own. I don't want to see that happen again in my family. Tell Tim.

He's a big boy and it will shock him, but he will be able to handle it. He will not leave you. Now, I need all of that paperwork before I can help you at all. You bring it and your family here on Saturday and we will see how bad it is. Are you clear on that?" Ti asked.

Reluctantly, Tricia agreed. Her head was spinning with the news of her father's debt and having to bring Tim. She wanted to keep this all a secret. Now she had to tell Tim everything. She wasn't sure what she was getting herself into.

Lessons from Chapter 2

Take Care of the Basics First

Take care of your family's basic needs first, regardless of what any credit card company says. You need a roof over your head, heat, water, and food: They come first. After that, prioritize the rest of your payments.

Keep Bookkeeping Simple

All you need is a spiral notebook for your household bookkeeping. You do not need complicated software or a scientific calculator. Get a notebook at the dollar store and start filling, from left to right, the date, nature or company name of the debit or deposit, and then the amount. If it is a debit, put a negative sign in front of it. In an hour, you can have a monthly total of what your surplus or shortfall is. Don't forget quarterly or annual items like insurance or property taxes. Just put it in monthly terms. In the Depression era, they called these ledgers. Don't make it more complicated than it needs to be.

Chapter 3 – The Truth Shall Set You Free

Tricia fretted the whole drive home. She had hoped that she would have money and Tim would never be the wiser. That wasn't going to happen, and she would have to tell him how bad it is. How do you tell your husband that you are in financial ruin? Tricia did not have the answer.

After putting the kids to bed, she joined Tim in the den. This was usually their time to share the day's events and catch up on what was happening in their lives. Tricia didn't know how to approach the subject so she asked about work instead. "What is the news at the plant? Any word on when they will get to full production?"

"It won't be for a while, I'm afraid," Tim answered without looking up. "The whole second line is still down. I am lucky to be working at all."

"I know. I do feel grateful that you were one of the first to go back. All that extra training last year paid off." Tricia paused for a moment and then blurted, "I went to see my grandmother today."

"Oh," said Tim looking up. "And what do we owe this occasion to?"

"I asked her for a loan."

The silence that followed seemed to last forever. Tricia could not look up; the tears started streaming down her face. How could she be such a bad person, and how will he ever love her again?

"What did you say?" he asked, jumping to his feet. "Look at me. You asked her for a loan? Why? What's going on?"

Tricia couldn't speak. She just looked at him and sobbed. He came to her and put his arms around her. He knew that her grandmother wasn't her favorite person, so it must be serious. He didn't know what to do or say.

Finally, Tim gently lifted Tricia's face up to look at him and said, "You need to tell me what's going on. I need to know."

Tricia slowly told him everything. She ended the confession repeating that she was sorry. She wondered if he would ever forgive her.

"You have to be kidding me. What have you done? What were you thinking? I am working my ass off and you are putting us in the poorhouse. I knew I should have been taking care of the money."

Tricia shuddered. This was exactly what she expected. This is why she couldn't tell him before. "I wanted to tell you. I thought once the house sold, I would be able to pay off everything and we could go back to normal."

"Well, that didn't happen, did it? You were spending money we didn't have. I was wondering what was going on. I knew that with my layoff we should have been short of cash, but I trusted you. I trusted you to take care of it."

Tim stormed out of the room. Tricia didn't know whether to follow or to stay where she was. He had a temper, and she didn't like it when he was all wound up.

Tim didn't even look at her for the rest of the day. Every time she approached him, he would walk away. She finally went up to the bedroom and cried herself to sleep. All she could think about was the article she had read the week before. It outlined the top reasons for divorce; money was number one. Now she knew why.

The next day, Tim went to work without speaking to her. Tricia did not know what to do. She had no other alternative but to go to her grandmother's on Saturday, and she couldn't go without him. As she drove the kids to school, she remembered the happiness she had enjoyed on Parkside. She couldn't stop hating herself for ruining everything.

She went through the day in a daze and barely made it through the supper hour and putting the kids to bed. She finished cleaning the kitchen and went to bed exhausted. A few minutes later, Tim walked into the room and turned on the bedside lamp. "I didn't know it was this bad. It just makes me so angry to think we are nearly bankrupt after working so hard for the past ten years. I am having a hard time not blaming you for everything. I was wondering where all the money was coming from, but you looked so confident and I wanted to believe that everything was just fine. I know I am paying a price for putting my head in the sand. I should have been trying to help. I don't know if we can get through this, but I will try. Let's start by selling this damn house."

"Even if we sold it, we would still have debt left over, and with rent, I don't know if our cash flow would be much better. I think we have to get out of this mess from here. I don't know how, but my grandmother promised she would show us. Will you go with me on Saturday?" Tricia asked quietly.

"Why would we talk to her? She has been so mean to you. Why not go to the mortgage broker and look at refinancing or something?"

"I tried that. No one will lend us money. Why do you think I went to her? I found out why she was so distant. It wasn't her. It was my dad. He felt bad because he owed her money. That is why we only went on Christmas Eve. I guess he felt he owed her that much. There was so much I didn't know about my family. I don't want to repeat that here. She wants me to make a list of everything. Can you go through it with me? If you see it bit by bit, you won't be so shocked. It is bad."

"I guess we could do it tomorrow after work. I don't want to be like your parents, or mine for that matter. I just still can't get past why you didn't tell me."

"I didn't want you to leave me." Tricia started to cry.

"I am not going to leave," Tim said as he walked over to her side of the bed.

She felt as if this huge weight had been lifted off her shoulders. She hadn't realized how hard it had been to carry that secret around or how much she feared Tim leaving her. His support gave her a newfound incentive to take care of this problem now. Whatever her grandmother said, she would do. Her family was too important to let them down anymore.

When Tricia started to gather the information her grandmother had requested, she found it was worse than she thought. They had almost $49,000 in credit card debt. Their mortgage, at $235,000, was more than the house was worth now and their expenses were almost $1,600 a month more than their income. When she finished, she didn't think anyone would be able to help them out of this mess.

Lesson from Chapter 3

The Truth Shall Set You Free

You need to identify and accept reality first and then be open and honest with those in your family. Living a lie takes so much energy. Until you are ready to tell the truth and get the help you need, you cannot move forward. Do not let fear stand in your way. Trust your partner and those around you to accept the truth. There is no other way.

You also need to be truthful with your creditors. Shame often keeps us from letting others know that we are in trouble. If your creditors know the truth, they are more apt to work with you to find a solution.

Once you have been honest with yourself and others, you can begin to work on fixing the problem. Remember, you have to find the starting line before you can run the course.

Chapter 4 – There Is No Easy Way Out

Tricia went over the details with Tim on the Friday night so he would know everything before she revealed it all to her grandmother. He looked like his world had ended. Tricia had not prepared him for this. What were they going to do? She did not want to lose her house. She did not want to lose her family. She knew life was going to change drastically.

Saturday morning, the weather was dull and gray with pockets of fog. The weather reflected how Tricia felt. Tim and Tricia did not speak a word over breakfast, and even the kids were unusually quiet. Tricia looked around her dream house as they left and wondered what she had done. Was this house worth it?

At her grandmother's, the silence was heavy. The kids had a table set up in the kitchen full of crayons and paper and were not making a sound as they worked on their pictures. Ti was looking over the documents that Tricia had given her, and Tim looked off into space.

After a look at all the paperwork they had brought, Ti looked up. "Well, it is fixable. It will take hard work and a total change in lifestyle. Would you consider selling the house?"

"That would be the last resort," Tim answered quickly.

Tricia looked at him in surprise. She thought he would have jumped at the chance to get rid of the house after their previous conversation. Even Tricia was ready to give it all up to have her life back.

"Are you sure?" asked Tricia. "I will do anything to take care of this, so if she thinks selling the house will help, I will."

"If we have to, we will. Can we try to fix this without selling the house?" Tim directed the question at Ti.

"It makes it more difficult, but if you commit to fixing this, we may be able to keep the house. That will be your only luxury for a while though, I'm afraid. We will need to slash your monthly expenses and then we will look at ways to increase your income. The two of you have your work cut out for you. You are spending almost twice as much as you make. Do you see how quickly this is adding up? In five years, you will have over $200,000 in credit card debt if you keep on going in the same direction. That doesn't even include your mortgage. Do you understand the seriousness of this?"

Both Tim and Tricia remained quiet. They knew it was bad when they looked at the numbers at home, but the thought of all of that debt overwhelmed them. Tricia started to cry.

Tim looked at her and said, "I can't believe this. I guess the only thing you did right was to call in an expert." He sounded angry and the words came out in a hiss.

"Well, isn't this swell, blaming her. You didn't have a hand in this at all? You had no more respect for money than she did. This problem is too big for one person to have made. You need to face that fact and stop being such a coward." Ti stood there with her hands on her hips and glared at Tim.

"You *would* want to protect her. I didn't know it was this bad. How could it be my fault?" Tim stood as well and looked ready to leave.

"Did you ask about your finances? Did you even bother to find out what was happening? In the courts, ignorance is not a defense and the same stands true in my house. You left her to do everything and she did. Did she make the right choices? No, she did not. But neither did you by ignoring the problem."

Tim slumped back down in his chair. He knew she was right. It was easier to blame Tricia than to think about how stupid he had been. He didn't want to admit this. It devastated him to admit how badly off they were. He thought of all the years of hard work and he didn't know how to deal with it.

"So why don't we just declare bankruptcy and get it over with? I don't believe we are going to get out of this. What do we have to do to make it go away?" Tim asked in defeat.

"Bankruptcy seems easy, but it's not. It is short-term gain for long-term pain. And it isn't as easy as it used to be to declare bankruptcy. If you do, you may get rid of the bills, but you will have the emotional and financial scars to deal with for a long time. If you've slashed your expenses and are making as much income as possible and still can't balance your budget, it is time to consider professional counseling or bankruptcy. Until then, you are going to have to work hard to make up that money, even if it means giving up many of the pleasures of life to do it."

Ti knew this was not what Tim wanted to hear. He wanted it all to go away, and that wasn't going to happen. They would feel the financial effects for years to come, whether they declared bankruptcy or not. She waited for her words to sink in a little before she continued. "I know you just want this all to go away, but it isn't going to. There is no easy way. There is no 'Thirty Days to Debt-free.' You may see that advertised, but most if it is just rubbish. They can charge you various fees and you will still have a big black mark against your credit. The only way to tackle this and have a good life to look forward to is to pay back what you owe and to start taking control of what's left. There is no instant solution. You have a choice right now. You can try to make it right. And you can choose to do it and have fun. Ever see the show by National Geographic that covers the poorest parts of the world? The kids have nothing, sometimes not even something to eat, but many of them are smiling and laughing and having fun. I think about that a lot, and it helps me to stop feeling sorry for myself. Some of my fondest memories are from when I didn't have much money, because not having money simplifies life. I hope you will see the good side of that," Ti said with all the emotion that comes from a lifetime of experience. "You don't let life make you happy; you make a happy life with whatever you have to do it with. Do either of you get what I am saying?"

"I do, Grammy Ti, but I just feel so guilty and angry. I blame myself for this and I just want to curl up in a ball and make it all go away. How do I deal with all this?" Tricia could not control her emotions any longer, and she started to cry again.

Ti got up and walked over to her. "Patricia, guilt never did anyone any good. You just have to forgive yourself and move on. You will find fixing this problem will make you a stronger and better person. I know you can do this. Your generation was handed everything. It is a blessing that you have never known hunger or known what it was like to want something very much, with no practical way of getting it. But it is a shame that you have never felt the satisfaction of saving for years and forgoing everything else until you have enough money to get it. It makes you appreciate everything so much more. When you get it in an instant, you miss all the joy of thinking and dreaming about it."

"I feel the same way as you, Trish," Tim said. "I just don't know what to do with this anger. I want this to be a bad dream, but it's not. So we have to do it together. I'm sorry I blamed it all on you."

Tim didn't move closer to Tricia but his eyes were pleading with her to forgive him. The room was silent for a few moments. Ti knew these two had to accept responsibility and move on, and she was willing to wait for that to happen. She wasn't even sure if she could help them out of this. They had done a great job at making bankruptcy look inviting.

"It's okay," Tricia said. "I made this mess, so I am willing to fix it."

"We're going to fix it. Bankruptcy is not the answer for us," Tim added as he moved over to the couch and held Tricia's hand.

Lessons from Chapter 4

Stop Feeling Sorry for Yourself

Feeling sorry for yourself is a waste of time and energy. You need to focus on what you can change, and leave the rest to God. He will always meet you halfway.

Lack of Money Simplifies Life

When you do not have much money, life gets simpler because you have limited choices. You may see this as negative, but it can be a positive. In the Depression, fond memories came from simple times spent together. Families listened to the radio, read out loud to one another, and had fun working together on chores. None of these takes money. Think about playing cards, reading a library book, playing charades, or telling funny stories. Money doesn't buy happiness or memories.

Appreciation

My mother grew up in Newfoundland in the Depression era. If you ask her about Christmas, she will tell you about getting an orange in her stocking when she was a small child. You couldn't get fruit in the winter like you can today, so it was a rare delicacy. That was almost seventy years ago, but you can still see the delight in her face when she talks about that small token in her stocking. How many of us can remember what we received last year for Christmas, let alone decades ago? It is hard to appreciate anything when there is too much of it and it comes to us easily.

We have robbed our children of the joy and anticipation they would feel if they saved up for something they wanted. We are under such pressure to make them happy that we miss the opportunity to allow them to wait and save for what they want. They will appreciate it a lot longer if they saved and sacrificed for it than if you handed it to them.

Chapter 5 – Cutting Expenses

Ti was happy that both Tricia and Tim were on the same page. She knew that this was going to take work, and if they both weren't fully on board, there would be no happy ending.

"Okay, back to business then. Do you both agree that keeping the house is your only luxury?" Ti asked.

"Yes," they answered together, and Ti moved on.

"We could save a few hundred dollars a month if we sell the house, and there may even be some equity to reduce your debts. But if you want to keep it, let's look at everything else. Let's take a good look at your expenses. Eating out is no longer a choice. In fact, your food bill is one of your biggest expenses. You will only have half of that amount in your new budget."

"How the heck are we going to do that?" Tricia asked feeling panicked. "It is not like we eat steak every night, and the kids get a big kick out of going to McDonald's. I'll agree to give up our Friday night date, but do we have to give up everything?"

"I will say it again: the only luxury you may have is your home. What is your kids' favorite meal at home?"

"Hot dogs, I guess," said Tricia reluctantly.

"Kyle and Sophie, what if you have hot dogs and french fries at home on Friday nights and your parents played cards with you?" she asked, interrupting their coloring at the kitchen table.

"You would play cards with us, Mommy? Scott taught me how

to play Crazy 8s and I am pretty good. Can we, Mommy?" asked Kyle.

"Sure," replied Tricia and then turned to Ti. "Is this why you made me bring the kids? You want more reinforcements for your arguments?"

"No. Children need to know that you can deal with money without going crazy. Most kids either think money grows on trees or it is evil. They learn this from their parents. Don't you want your kids to grow up and be responsible with their money?"

"Of course I do," said Tricia. "I don't ever want them to go through what I'm going through now."

"Then let's keep going. As for your date night, you can still have date night every Friday. It will be different. You don't need to go out. Feed the kids their hot dogs and play cards with them and then put them to bed. Then you two can sit down to a nice meal and enjoy each other's company. Between McDonald's and your date night, you were spending about $75 each week. Now you are spending less than $20, including a bottle of wine. Your kids will be happy and you should be happy too."

"You know, it always bothered me to pay just as much in babysitting as it did on the meal," said Tim. "I would like to have a relaxing dinner at home. What do you think, honey?"

"It was my one night out of the house, so I won't lie to you and say I won't miss it. I guess as long as we get to spend some time alone, it will be all right. We can even cook together—try some new dishes."

"Well, that was easier than I thought," said Ti. "I expected a battle, but I see you *are* ready to change this. So the grocery bill is coming down. It won't hurt you to eat grilled cheese sandwiches and hot dogs for a while. When I was a kid, I would have thought I had died and gone to heaven with that menu," she said with a laugh.

Tricia had no memory of her grandmother laughing before. She had always seemed distant and unhappy when they went to visit her, and Tricia believed she was incapable of laughing. She realized that she didn't know her grandmother at all. She didn't know anything about her grandmother's childhood or what her great-grandparents were like.

"The next item we need to chop is not going to make you happy, Patricia. The housekeeper is gone. You are all going to have to chip in and clean your own house. When I was working, I would always get everyone cleaning on Thursday night. That way, when I came home from a long week of work on Friday, my house looked great. We would sing and dance while we scrubbed and cleaned. I have some fond memories of your dad dancing with a broom. He would make me laugh until I cried. It was one of my favorite times of the week." Ti stopped and stared off into space.

Tricia could see her father being crazy and dancing like that, and it brought tears to her eyes. She looked over at her grandmother and saw that she too was thinking of her father. "I miss him," Tricia said quietly.

Ti, startled out of her daydream, looked at Tricia. She patted her hand and said, "So do I, Patricia."

It took Ti a few moments to get back on topic. It had been a long time since she had thought about her son when he was a young boy. She had almost forgotten how much fun they used to have as a family. She snapped her mind back into the present and tried to get back on track. She had a list of the expenses and she kept checking it over.

"Well, do you have anything to say about letting the housekeeper go, Patricia?" Ti asked with a look that dared her to make a comment. Tricia caught on and shook her head. "Good. The next item on the agenda is the cars. Tim, don't you work at Fairfax? Isn't that just a few blocks from your house?"

"I guess. It is about a ten-minute walk, if that's what you're getting at," Tim replied.

"So, you have a car payment that you could do without if you walked to work. What do you think that car is worth?"

"I could probably get $4,000 to $4,500. It only costs $250 a month, and I only have fourteen payments until it is all paid off. I don't want to sell it," Tim said with dismay.

"Then sell the house," Ti suggested with little emotion.

"Okay, okay. There was a guy asking about it at work. He knows I am crazy about keeping my car maintained, and he needs a new one. Like the rest of us, he doesn't have much money, though."

"See what you can do. You would save $250 a month and have money left over to pay some of this debt. If the weather is ugly, Patricia could always drop you off. Just so you know, I used to walk three blocks to the bus stop and then ride the bus for twenty minutes when I worked downtown. It never hurt me. You don't have the money to pay for the gas and insurance. In fact, you don't have any money to go anywhere in your car," she said with a smile.

Tricia almost believed that she winked. Again, the sparkle she saw in her grandmother's eye shocked her. This was not the woman she remembered.

"Having one car is scary to me. Do we have to be that drastic?" Tim asked. "Tricia's car has quite a few miles on it and I am not sure how long it is going to last."

"Unfortunately, the answer is yes. You have to be drastic. There is no room for wants; only needs. You don't *need* a second car. Someday you will be able to afford the luxury of a second car. You two have a reliable one to get you through right now. Remember, some people don't even have one car."

"I know, but this is hard. I didn't think you were going to take my car. I can't pretend to be happy about that," Tim said glumly.

"Let's get this straight: I am not *taking* your car from you. You are deciding that it is best for your family to have one car. You don't have to do any of this. In fact, you are technically bankrupt, at least on paper, so you don't own anything at all. Do you get that?"

"I get it."

"Patricia?"

"Yes, I get it."

It surprised Tricia that Tim would have to sell his car. He loved that car and spent every Saturday cleaning it and checking the oil. Tricia would kid him that he paid more attention to the car than he did to his own wife. She knew this was going to be hard for him, and she felt guilty that he was going to pay the price for her financial mismanagement.

"Let's keep going." Ti was on to the next item on the list. "Now, what is this $10 a week at Karner's Variety?"

"That is my lottery tickets. I have been buying them there for the last five years. I can't stop now," Tim said in a strained voice. "The car

Cutting Expenses

is one thing to give up. But you want me to give up my $10? You've got to be kidding me."

"Just think about this now. You have spent $10 each week for the last five years. How much have you won?"

"I haven't won anything but a free ticket now and then. But if I don't play, my numbers will surely come up and then I will lose my mind," Tim replied defiantly.

"You'll lose your house before then," Ti quickly answered. "Let's see, $10 each week for five years. That is over $2,500, not including interest. Wouldn't you love to have $2,500 sitting in the bank right now? I will tell you what: It costs $1 a play. You can buy one ticket a week."

Tim was furious. She cut out everything he had fun with. He didn't do anything wrong, yet he was the one punished. "I am not happy right now, Trish. My fun is gone. What's wrong with this picture? I thought a little budgeting would be fine. Maybe I couldn't buy coffee at work every day and you couldn't go shopping and buy clothes for the kids that they don't need. I didn't think I would have to sell my car - and playing the lottery is the only fun I have."

"You know, Tim, I think you have your life all wrong. You are only looking at it as it revolves around you. You are missing out if lottery tickets are your only fun. Play ball with your kids. Dance in the kitchen with your wife. Watch football with your buddies. You need to get rid of that car so you can see all of what you're missing," Ti said with emotion. "It goes by so fast. Next thing you know, your kids are gone and you are wondering what to do with yourself. It makes it a little easier if you have some memories to look back on. You will not want a clean car and a free lotto ticket to be the only memories you have."

"Tim, I am sorry. I just thought we would be so much happier in our new house that I was blind to what it may cost and what may happen to you. I do want to spend more time with you, and I am sure the kids would love it too. I will drive you to work every day if you want." Tricia couldn't stop the tears now. "What do you want to do?"

"Well, I want to get out of this mess, but I didn't think it would be like this. I'll agree to follow your grandmother's plan for six months.

I figure I can do anything, knowing it will stop in six months. If there isn't some real headway made on this disaster, than I am going to pull the plug. Agreed?" Tim looked directly at Tricia.

"Agreed," said Tricia quietly.

She didn't know how to feel. She felt excited at first when it looked as if her grandmother could help them. She was a little disappointed about date night, but she was already thinking about fun meals they could make together. It might be more romantic at home in candlelight than in a busy restaurant. When Tim had started yelling, her stomach turned. She had thought he was on board. Now she wondered if they could make a difference in six months.

"Are we ready to move on?" Ti interrupted the silence. "Next on the list is shopping. Do you know how much you have been spending on clothes for the family? I know kids grow, but this is ridiculous. For the next sixty days, no new clothes for anyone. You can patch knees, darn socks, or do whatever you have to. No more clothes. I realize that in two months, one or both of the kids may move up a size. When they are growing like weeds, you don't buy a lot at one time and you don't spend a lot. Have you been down to Via's Values? I went last week and there are clothes for a dollar that still have the sales tags on them. It is worth it for play clothes, and you can find all kinds of bargains."

"You've got to be kidding. I wouldn't be caught dead in there. What if someone I knew saw me in there?" Tricia grimaced.

"Once the sixty days is up, you will have $50 a month for the whole family's clothing budget. You may change your mind." Ti couldn't help smiling when she said this. She knew how some people felt about buying used items. They hadn't lived through the Depression, so they did not have an appreciation for a good bargain. Via's Values gave people an opportunity to buy used clothes at a deep discount. They gave their profits to several different charities, so it helped the whole community. "I'll tell you what: I will take you down there and help you look, and if anyone sees you, you can tell them you are taking your poor old grandmother out to shop," Ti said with a laugh. "I'll have you hooked on bargain hunting before you know it. Now, after all of this hard work, I think we deserve a coffee break. Don't you?"

Cutting Expenses

They all headed into the kitchen to check on the kids and warm up their coffee. Ti knew they would need some reinforcements before tackling the next subject.

Lessons from Chapter 5

If It Was Easy, Everyone Would Do It

Giving up material things you love is not easy. But they are only things. As a society, we have become confused and now believe they are what bring us happiness. Don't delay happiness for a future purchase or event. Enjoy today with whatever you have.

It will be hard for you to go to one car. It will be hard to say no to your kids, really hard. It will be hard to tell someone that you can't because you don't have the money. But it will get easier.

Why Not Borrow?

In the Depression, people swapped clothes and equipment. It was not feasible to own every item you would possibly use in a year, so neighbors pooled their resources. Nothing went to waste.

This year, my daughters borrowed their semi-formal dresses. They were upset that they had to, until they found out that many of their friends borrowed dresses as well. They shared accessories and purses. They all found beautiful outfits, and I stayed on budget. It was hard for me to admit that I couldn't afford to buy them, but I realized it was a waste to buy a dress for a teenager for one night. Borrowing was a better solution.

Try having a party where everyone brings clothes to trade. This works well if you have a group with kids of various ages, so the clothes one child has outgrown are passed down to a younger child. Even adults can exchange clothes. Think about the clothes at the back of your closet with the tags still on them. It can be a fun social evening with a purpose.

Exchange bigger items as well. You can look at exchanging tools or renting them, instead of buying them outright. We buy tools for one job and then they sit in the garage. Rent instead. Or, ask your neighbor about pooling your resources. You will save money as well as space.

Need versus Want

Credit blurs the line between *need* and *want*. When you have a limited cash budget, it becomes much clearer. In the first stages, you need to recognize there will be no luxuries. This is not forever. But for now, you will only look at what you need. Paying the electric bill is a need. The cable bill or cell phone is not. Buying required textbooks for school is a need. Having brand-new textbooks is not. Can you do without it? That is the single most important question to ask oneself, whether you can, delay, defer, or delete the item from your list.

Chapter 6 – Beating Credit Card Bullies

"Now, we have dealt with food, housekeeper, cars, lottery tickets, and clothing. We are really cutting off the fat. You guys will be living lean, and soon you won't even notice the difference. Next on my list are those credit cards. I looked at your minimum payment and your interest costs. The payment barely covers the interest. It will take you twenty years to pay them off at this rate. This is what you need to do. You need to call all the companies and ask them to lower your rate. Have you been paying on time?" Ti asked.

"Most of the time, I guess," replied Tricia. "I am usually behind a month on at least one because I just don't have the money."

"That can hurt you. Some companies will hold that against you. But we can work around that. So, you need to call these companies and ask them to lower your interest rate. Look up what some of the offers are out there and tell them you are going to move your business to another company at a lower rate if they don't change theirs. Now you may get a song and dance. The first answer may be a no. Your job is to keep going until you get a yes. Ask for a supervisor. Ask for their supervisor. Keep asking until someone says yes. If the threat to move to another company doesn't work, you may have to tell them about your budget and let them know without their cooperation, you won't be able to pay at all. This is a conversation to be had with someone who has the authority to help you. Once we know what the companies agree to, we will look at a repayment schedule."

"I am nervous about phoning these guys, Grammy Ti. They keep calling and telling me that if I don't do exactly as they say, I am going to lose my house and my family. They even called me at work the other day and threatened to tell my boss. I was only behind forty-five days."

"Let's go over the rules, because they do have rules to follow. They can't tell your boss or anyone else, because of the laws to protect your privacy. They can't call you anytime of the day or night. There is a limit on how early and late they can call. They can't have you arrested or take away your house. When they call and threaten you, tell them you are going to take down their name and report them if they ever call you again. If they threaten you again, tell them they have broken the law and you will sue them. They're not expecting that, because they are bullies and want everyone to be afraid of them. We are going to get you caught up on your payments, and this will all stop. Once we lower your interest, you will be able to pay it all off even faster. So I want you to take care of each of the credit card companies before you come back next Saturday."

"Next Saturday?" Tricia looked puzzled.

"You didn't think I would be able to settle the crisis of your life in one afternoon, did you? This is going to take some time, I am afraid. So you will have to come back for a couple of weeks at least," Ti said, looking serious, but Tricia still noticed a little twinkle in her eye.

"I am old, and all this thinking has tired me out. How about some lunch? Kids, are you getting hungry yet?" Ti yelled into the kitchen as she got up.

Kyle and Sophie looked up from their artwork. Ti had given the children glue and sparkles, a box of fifty different crayons, colored paper, and special scissors used for scrapbooking. Tricia had never seen them sit for so long and hardly make a sound. The kitchen table was a mess, but Tricia noticed that her grandmother had covered it with a clear plastic tablecloth so it would be easy to clean up.

"Well, Grammy Ti wants us to stay for lunch. Are you hungry?" Tricia asked.

"I'm starving," Kyle said and then went back to his picture.

"I don't want to stop coloring," Sophie whined. "Grammy, please don't make me stop."

Ti walked over to the table. "How could I keep you from working on such a beautiful masterpiece? I will have everyone eat in the dining room, so you just have to stop long enough to eat. Will that work?"

Sophie nodded. She then bent back down over her paper and carefully painted the purple band in her rainbow. Tricia was a little embarrassed that she did not do crafts with her kids. She had never thought of it. The weekends were a whirlwind of shopping and laundry. Tricia realized that she never did any activities with them regularly. She made a mental note to have her grandmother include a few dollars a week to go to the dollar store to buy craft supplies.

They sat down to a lunch of homemade soup and sandwiches. Ti told the kids stories of her mother making a half dozen loaves of bread every week and eating hot bread with melted butter. She also told them about helping her father make beer in an old crock covered with cheesecloth in the cold cellar. Everyone laughed when Sophie asked how they made cloth out of cheese. Tricia had never thought of her grandmother as a young girl. It never dawned on her that her grandmother had a life before she married and had children. She realized she was enjoying the stories as much as the kids were.

"Well," Tim said, "we had better get going. I have a car to clean." The kids groaned and rolled their eyes. Tricia and Ti exchanged a look of puzzlement. "So I can sell it," he added and they all laughed.

"Can we come back?" asked Sophie.

"Anytime you like, sweetie. You are coming back next Saturday for sure, though. Isn't that right, Patricia?" Ti looked at Tricia and grinned.

Tricia couldn't help smiling back. "Sure, Grammy Ti. Should we come at the same time?"

"That works for me. You still game, Tim?"

Tricia knew for sure this time that her grandmother had winked. Her grandmother, who had scared her half to death when she was a child, was winking at her husband. This could not be the same woman.

"I'm only coming back for the food, you know. You could bribe anyone with that soup," Tim said with a wink and then smiled at

Tricia. "I guess I'm trading my car in for good old-fashioned cooking. Not a bad trade."

Tricia knew at that moment that they were going to be fine. Tim melted under her grandmother's spell and he seemed pleased to be coming back. Three hours ago, Tricia had thought her life was over and the agony of visiting her mean old grandmother was her punishment for not taking care of her family. What a difference now. She too was looking forward to next Saturday.

As they walked out the door, Ti reminded Tim and Tricia of their budget constraints and their homework. She told Tim that he was responsible for calling two of the credit card companies, as was Tricia. They both needed the experience and the involvement. Tricia was thankful. She did want Tim involved. It was a lighter load with him helping her. She was also grateful that the rules didn't come from her. She had a feeling that Tim would not have been as cooperative if it was she who had told him to give up the car and lottery tickets.

Lessons from Chapter 6

The Credit Crunch

We have read and heard about the comparison between the current financial crisis and the Great Depression. There are many similarities, but we must remember that they did not have credit cards in the 1930s. It is different today because there are many people dealing with bankruptcy and foreclosure who still have jobs. That is a direct result of the easy credit we have enjoyed over the last few years.

That has all changed. Tightening of credit in the financial world has trickled down to the consumer. Rates are increasing even though governments around the world are lowering their prime rates. You need to do everything possible to protect yourself and become independent of credit today.

Credit Card Companies Have Rules to Follow

Find out what the laws are in your country, province, or state surrounding credit card companies and debt collectors. These laws are there to protect you, so use them. Do not be afraid of these companies. Know your rights and you will have a sense of empowerment that will help you deal with them on a fair playing field.

When dealing with each company, talk to a supervisor. They have the power to negotiate. Don't take *no* for an answer. They want your business as much as you want a lower rate.

Chapter 7 – Keep Asking until They Reduce Your Rate

They spent the next week revamping their banking and working out a budget, as well as contacting each of the credit card companies. Both Tricia and Tim felt uncomfortable making the phone calls. Tricia found the first company reluctant to do anything. They reminded her of her late payment two months ago and told her that she had known the interest rate when she applied for the card. This fifteen-minute conversation frustrated Tricia. She asked if there was anything she could do to lower it and the answer she got was no.

On the second call, Tricia was a little more successful. The representative pointed out the late payments and explained that if she paid her minimum balance on time for the next three months, she could apply to have her interest rate lowered. He reminded her that they would do a credit check then to make sure all of her payments were prompt. Tricia wrote down his name and employee number, as well as the date and time.

Tim found dealing with the credit card companies frustrating. He thought the companies would be eager to help them. They were trying to pay down their cards, and the high interest was slowing that down. It did not occur to him that they liked Tim having a large balance on the account because they were making money from the interest.

The first company would not lower the rate, but they suggested he call back in six months and they would review it. Tim decided that he was going to call them every month and try to get the rate reduced. It couldn't hurt. The second company was much more cooperative. They offered to change to a lower-rate card that also had no annual fee. The new interest rate would be effective immediately, so they were saving money right away.

Tim and Tricia compared notes. One out of four wasn't great odds, so they decided they would follow Ti's advice and keep trying. Tricia called back her first card company. She asked for a supervisor right away. She wouldn't waste any more of her time. She explained the plan they were developing to repay all of their debt. Tricia told her that she did not want to file for bankruptcy, and if the company cooperated, they would be able to get through these difficult times. The supervisor agreed to cut her interest rate in half. She did warn Tricia that if there were any more late payments, it would be increased to the higher rate again. Tricia thanked her and hung up. She started dancing and hollering. She could not believe that she had done that. She had managed to get the interest rate changed and it wasn't that hard.

"I can't believe the way you were talking on the phone," Tim said. "That was awesome."

"I can't believe it either. I was shaking when I started, but then I got into it and I decided I was not going to stop until that rate went down. I feel on top of the world right now."

"Great job, hon. Now, do it again while you are on this high," Tim laughed.

Tricia called the second company, but the supervisor told the same three month story. He explained that she had been late too many times and they needed to see a commitment to them before they would help her out. Tricia asked if they could do it in two months instead and the supervisor agreed. In addition, Tricia got him to take her off the contact list so no one would bother her again.

"I still say that is a success, Trish. We make the next two payments on time and then we get our rate lowered. Also, you stopped the phone calls. Good work," Tim said.

"Now it's your turn, Tim. It is actually fun."

"I don't know about that. My stomach is a little queasy."

"You'll be fine. Let me know how it goes. I'll be in the kitchen with the kids."

Tim dialed the phone. He couldn't believe how nervous he was. He also asked for a supervisor right away. He told him he was prepared to move to another company if they did not lower his rate. The supervisor told him the best he could do was to move him from 22 to 17 percent. He also waived the annual fee, so Tim saw the call as a victory.

Tim went to find Tricia to discuss the results. She told him how proud of him she was, and they discussed how great it felt taking back some control. When looking at the new rates of the four companies, they noticed the company that was the most reluctant to lower their rate was also the one with the highest interest rate. They decided that this would be the one that they would concentrate on paying down the fastest. Tricia vowed she would get rid of that debt.

They ranked all the cards in the order they would pay them off and both felt better having a strategy. Now, whenever there was extra money, it would go to the BNX card until it was at zero. Both the CSC Bank and the National Bank card had the same rate. They owed more on the CSC, so they decided they would go after the smaller balance next. When they finished paying BNX, they would use that money and add it to the minimum payment of the National Bank card so it would speed up paying it off. Because the Corporate Capital card now had the lowest interest cost, they would pay it off last. But by that time, they would have a lot each month to put toward it with all the extra money. They thought that this was the best plan to attack their credit card debt.

Both Tim and Tricia felt empowered having a plan. In the past, Tricia had struggled to keep everything afloat. Each month, the stress of it grew. Now she didn't even have to think about it. They paid their minimum payments to all the cards, and the extra went to BNX. She was eager to see the balances start to go down. She was almost giddy, thinking about it. They both talked about how it would feel when this debt was gone. They weren't building a shopping list of what they could buy when they no longer had these payments. Instead, they were figuring out how quickly their savings would grow at that pace.

Tim started laughing. "We have never saved a dime in our lives. Now that we are in a financial crisis, our dream is to save money. It's funny how life works, eh?"

"I know. I think it is just that we crave security. I want money in the bank from now on. I don't want to have to go through this again. I have learned my lesson. I thought I wouldn't be happy until we bought a house in Waverly. Look at us now. I look back at our little house on Parkside and I miss the simplicity of our life then. I didn't have a care in the world, it seemed," Tricia said as she pictured the house and sighed.

"I wouldn't say we didn't have a care in the world there. That is not exactly how I remember it. But it was easier. I am sure that with the fire at the plant, we would have had a little trouble anyway. Having two houses during my layoff just made it impossible. I have to say, though, I felt a lot like you did about wanting more. I dreamed about a new car, and I was thinking about adding on a garage. I also thought about building a huge play set in the back. I spent so much time wanting instead of appreciating what I had. I think this mess has taken the want out of me for a while."

"You're still going to have to watch me, because I am wired for shopping. I don't think the want is out of me yet," Tricia chuckled.

"You can go to Via's Values anytime you like and buy something for a buck. That should stop your need to shop for a while."

Tim laughed with Tricia and felt good about where they were. He knew that this was hard for her. Her parents spoiled her growing up, and shopping was the way she spent time with her mother. He also knew the commitment Trish had to fixing this, so he wasn't going to worry about her going out and blowing the budget. He also remembered that she was afraid of her grandmother, and that should keep her in check.

"Well, are you ready to set up the budget?" Tim asked.

"Let's do it. I want to make sure I set aside a little bit each week to buy craft supplies at the dollar store. Did you see how the kids loved it at Grammy Ti's?"

"What happened to *Crazy* Grammy Ti?" Tim asked with a raise of his eyebrow.

"She is so different from what I remembered. She scared me as a kid. I hated going there. Now that I know what was going on, it changes everything. She was so great with us and did you see how she was with Kyle and Sophie. I think the *Crazy* is gone for good. And as I recall, it was my mom who called her that. Can you believe she would do that?" A feeling of anger flashed in Tricia and she felt the need to defend her grandmother. She couldn't believe her mother had treated Grammy Ti like that.

"I, for one, am going back for the soup," Tim said with a laugh and then leaned over and kissed Tricia.

Both of them knew that going back next week was a good thing. They had progressed so much already. They were eager to work on the budget. After tackling the phone calls, they had the confidence they needed to finish off the rest of the work.

Lessons from Chapter 7

Dealing with Creditors

A creditor wants to be paid and will do what is necessary—including working with you—to keep you solvent. You need to deal with each company separately and spell out what you can do to make this work. Always deal with the person who has the authority to change the current agreement. Be clear about what you want and what you can do. Keep trying until you get the terms that work for you.

Have a Debt Repayment Plan that Makes Sense

If you have a limited budget, you need to be smart. If you do not have enough to pay all of your minimum payments, see if the credit card companies will temporarily agree to you just paying interest until you can increase your income. Agree on the payment so you can stop the phone calls. Corporations that know you are working on a plan to pay them are more apt to give you the time to put it in place.

If you have enough to pay, you need to be systematic. Pay all the minimums and then put the excess toward the card with the highest interest rate. If you have two with the same rate, put the excess on the one with the lowest amount owing. When it's paid, take its minimum payment amount with the excess and apply it to the next-highest-interest card. Keep going until they are all paid off.

We often fall prey to the "squeaky wheel gets the grease" syndrome. If a particular company is badgering you, you want to pay them off as quickly as possible to get rid of them. That may make sense emotionally, but it could be wrong financially. Putting this plan in place takes the emotion out of it and makes it easy for you to benefit financially.

Chapter 8 – Having Fun for Free

Tricia was struggling with the food budget. She didn't want grilled cheese and hot dogs. How was she going to make decent meals with a limited amount of money? She decided to go online and see if there were any recipes that were cheap but nutritious. She found a couple of Web sites that had exactly what she was looking for. She decided she would try alternating between cheap and really cheap, and see whether that would fit into the budget. She made out her grocery list and was curious to see if it she could make it work.

She knew she could stay on budget for clothing. The kids still had clothes they hadn't even worn for the first time. Sixty days wasn't long. She wasn't planning on buying at Via's, but she would go to satisfy her grandmother. She hadn't needed anything for years, but she enjoyed shopping so much she would buy clothes anyway. Those days were over.

She thought it was time to let her housekeeper know she was no longer needed. Tricia hated cleaning the house, and it would be a tough phone call to make. She went to the kitchen to find the number and saw Tim on the phone. He was at the kitchen table with paper and pen, looking serious. Tricia wondered what was going on. As she came closer, she could hear Tim say he couldn't take less than $4,500 and she knew. Poor Tim was selling his car. She stood in the doorway out of sight.

"You know, I just changed the brake pads and the tires. Do you know how much that cost me and how much it will save you?" Tim asked his friend Charlie over the phone. "You are getting a bargain. When I put it in the newspaper, I'll be asking $5,000. I am giving you a break."

When Tim hung up, Tricia walked over to him. "Well? What happened?"

"He's going to let me know tomorrow at work. He has to go over his finances to see if he can afford it. I couldn't pressure him knowing how it feels to buy something you can't afford. If he won't buy it, someone else will. It is a great car." Tim walked over to the fridge and grabbed a beer. "It isn't easy though, Trish."

"I know, Tim. It breaks my heart. What if we make saving for a car one of our goals? You always wanted a Corvette to work on. Just knowing that it's a possibility for the future may be worth it. What do you think?"

"You know, even if I had a dollar a week toward a Corvette, I could at least dream. I could also shop and compare prices, so when I am ready in a couple of years to buy, I'll be an expert. I feel a little bit better already."

"A dollar a week it is. I will put that into the budget. You have that old cigar box in your bottom drawer. You can use that. Just think, in a couple of months you will be able to afford that bumper sticker 'Life begins in a Corvette.' You can hang it up in the garage and dream about it while you're out there working on my car," Tricia joked. Tim smiled up at her. Tricia realized that over the past six months, there hadn't been much laughing or smiling going on. It felt good to kid him. It felt good to see him smile.

"You think you're being smart, but I think it is a good idea," Tim said, beaming. "It will keep me focused on the long term and not worry about what I am missing now. I will own a Corvette. I am excited about it. It doesn't matter if it takes me five years or ten. Just knowing I am saving money for it makes me happy. What do you want, Tricia?" He looked over at her and his voice took a serious tone.

"You know, if you had asked me six months ago, I would have had a list. I can honestly say there isn't anything I want other than to pay off all these debts. It is the vision of a debt-free future that gets me excited. I have my dream home and my dream family. I realized that I have spent too much time buying stuff and too little time with you and the kids. Now I am focused on having the most fun with the least amount of money. My grandmother may be right. She may turn me into a bargain hunter after all."

She went over to him and hugged him. Facing this reality was hard, and she knew that living within their budget was not going to be easy. But for the first time in her life, she was thinking it was possible; she could do this. This was a big change for her.

Tricia broke the embrace. "We need to get back to work. I have done the food and clothing, and I was about to call Nell and break to the news to her." Tricia still wasn't looking forward to that phone call.

"Not yet. This feels great. I don't want to move from this spot. It seems so long since we have been alone together and smiling." Tim pulled her close and kissed her.

Tricia could not remember the last time they had been like this either. It felt great. She relaxed against him and let all the tension go. Neither moved; they enjoyed the closeness. It seemed like they stayed there forever.

"I will never call Nell if I don't do it now. This won't be an easy call."

"It is not as bad as you think. She may be a little upset, but she'll understand. You will feel better after the call."

Tim left to find his cigar box, and Tricia turned to the phone. She wondered why this was so hard for her. Was she embarrassed that she could no longer afford a housekeeper? Also, without help around the house, she wondered how she was going to do it all. Adding housework into her life seemed overwhelming. She shook her head and chastised herself out loud, "Quit being such a princess. You are being a big suck and that has to stop."

Kyle came around the corner and stared at her. "Who are you talking to, Mommy?" he asked.

"Just talking to myself, kiddo. Crazy adults do that sometimes. What are you doing?" Tricia realized that she hadn't seen the kids for at least a half hour. Her eyes narrowed and she asked him again, "What are you two up to?"

"We are making Grammy a card. She looked so sad when we

left. Sophie and I decided that if we each made a card with our pictures on it, she won't be sad when we leave the next time." Kyle looked very concerned. "Dad set us up on his computer. We are using this cool program where we can change the way our pictures look. You should see Sophie's."

"You know, I just have to make this phone call and I will come up and look. What do you think about me making a card for Grammy?"

"That would be great, Mom. Can we help you? We know how to do it, you know." Kyle was grinning from ear to ear.

"Sure, just give me five minutes."

Kyle ran up the stairs, and Tricia realized that she had not noticed that her grandmother had been sad when they were leaving. How did the kids pick up on that? She had been thinking that this was a real chore for her grandmother, but she could be wrong. Tricia was happy to think that this may have a positive impact on Grammy Ti as well. That gave her the strength she needed to go make the phone call.

Once she had finished, Tricia walked up to the alcove at the top of the stairs. She saw three bodies hunched over the computer. They were all laughing about something. She peeked over their heads and Tim turned around. "Well?"

"You know, Nell was fine. She said that she had thought that I would have called her awhile ago. If I ever need her, she is willing to come back, even if I just need her once in a while. That made it so much easier for me." Tricia's voice faded away as the display on the computer screen caught her eye. There she and Tim were, dressed as knights, their faces peeking out from the visors, with 'SAVERS' in bold letters written above.

"Do you get it?" asked Tim. "You know, instead of 'saviors' on white horses, we are 'savers' on white horses. I thought your grandmother would enjoy the humor behind it."

Tricia looked at the three of them. They were having a great time creating these cards. She pulled up the clothes hamper and sat down. "What if you had me as a princess and you were saving me? Then you could be Super Saver!"

The three of them started talking all at once, sharing their own opinions to add to the idea of Tricia as a princess. Then Sophie wanted to be a princess as well. Tricia began to realize that she was changing her image from saver to victim. She quickly discarded that idea. She would never play the role of victim again.

"I have changed my mind. I want to be the 'Super Saver' and Tim, you can be the princess. We could put you in a Corvette."

They all started laughing at her joke and soon they were giggling and carrying on, trying to come up with the funniest image. The final card had Tricia looking like Tarzan swooping down from a tree to rescue Tim. He looked like a princess sitting in a Corvette in King Kong's hand. The kids were monkeys hanging from the tree. It had taken them a few hours to perfect the image, but nobody minded because they were having such a good time.

Tim looked over at Tricia. "See? It doesn't cost a dime to have fun. I don't even mind being the princess in all of this."

Tricia smiled back at him. "And I will rescue you anytime, Princess. So who's hungry?"

The kids shouted loudly that they were hungry, and even Tricia's stomach was beginning to rumble, so they headed to the kitchen to make dinner.

Lesson from Chapter 8

Cheap Entertainment Straight from the Depression

- Daydreaming
- Reading
- Dress-up
- Storytelling
- Playing music
- Dancing
- Listening to the radio
- Playing cards or games
- Singing
- Talking
- Playing catch
- Going for a walk
- Drawing or painting
- Taking a bath
- Having a water fight
- Baking cookies
- Having a friend over for coffee
- Fishing
- Planting a garden
- Sewing and needlepoint
- Writing a letter

It doesn't take much, if any, money to have fun. You just need to be creative and have the right frame of mind.

Chapter 9 – Celebrate the Baby Steps

As the week progressed, they found they were running out of money in their food budget. Tricia was careful, but the kids went through milk like crazy, and her planned meals cost a little more than she had thought. She did not want to fail the first week, so she worked with what she had and made the kids drink water. Everything else was going fine. Tim had an offer of $4,300 for the car, and he was considering it seriously. After paying off the loan, he would have almost $1,000 to put toward the credit cards. The more he thought about it, the closer he was to accepting the offer. Also, a dollar for lottery tickets and a dollar for his Corvette satisfied his craving for entertainment more than he thought it would.

Saturday morning, they got in the car to go to Ti's house. They decided this would be the last trip in Tim's car. He would deliver it to the new owner on Monday. The kids were chatting in the back and giggling about the card they had made as a family. Tim stared ahead, lost in his own thoughts. Tricia knew he was trying to enjoy the last ride in his car. Tricia was looking forward to seeing her grandmother. She was proud of what they did this past week.

Ti was watching out the window for them. She wasn't sure they would show. She knew that she had been hard on them last week, but it was necessary. Big problems needed big solutions. Ti knew that this generation had it easy. They had no idea what it was like growing up in the Depression. She was sure they had never gone to bed hungry or even worse, known that their parents had gone hungry so the children could eat. She wondered how the week had gone at Tim and Tricia's. As the car pulled in, she could not hide her disappointment that it was Tim's car. She was sure he would have sold the car this week. *This was not going to go well,* she thought. They hadn't even completed the first step. Ti held open the door and watched as the kids came bounding out of the car.

"Grammy, Grammy! Wait until you see what we brought you!" Kyle yelled.

"Don't spoil the surprise," Sophie scolded. The both ran to her as fast as they could.

"Slow down, kids." Ti watched the kids stop with a fearful look on their faces, and she realized there was an edge to her voice. She did not want to punish the kids for her disappointment with their parents. In a softer voice, she added, "I don't want you to hurt yourself."

Tricia and Tim followed the kids in, and Tricia had noticed the irritation in her grandmother's voice. *I wonder what her problem is?* she thought. Then Tricia realized it didn't matter, because she was sure she would cheer up when she learned of the progress they had made. Tricia couldn't wait to tell her about their week.

Ti had set up a new craft for the kids. She had a white mask for each of them and told them they were going to make Mardi Gras masks. She had paint, feathers, beads, and sequins to glue to the mask so they could each make their own work of art. Ti was glad they had a big project to do, because she needed some private time with their parents.

"Well, I see you couldn't complete one of your first tasks. I knew you were going to have a hard time giving up that car, but didn't anything I said last week knock some sense into you, Tim?" Ti was having a hard time keeping her anger under control.

"I guess we are going to get right to it then. No *hello* and *how are you* to start us off this week?" Tim asked. "If you must know, we drove the car here because it is the last day I will own it. Is it too much to ask to have one last bit of fun?"

Ti sat down heavily. She had been wrong and she had jumped to conclusions without even asking what was going on. It was unlike her. She was good at keeping her emotions in check, and here she accused Tim angrily without even giving him a chance. This family was getting to her, and she was uncomfortable about it.

"I'm sorry, Tim. I wasn't sure if you would come and then you came in your car. I jumped to conclusions. That's not fair of me. I'm just nervous because I'm not sure if I have the ability to help you. I wasn't sure if you would take my advice seriously. I have been worrying about it all week." She looked directly at Tim. He couldn't help but feel sorry for her. It never dawned on either him or Tricia that this would be hard on her as well.

"Look, we were so excited to come here today, and now we have gotten off on the wrong foot. After our visit last week, we took a real hard look at ourselves. We realized that we both knew that we shouldn't be spending like we did, but we didn't look at the consequences. It was all about keeping up appearances and not sacrificing anything. Meanwhile, we were sacrificing our future and didn't even realize it. We need your help. In one week, we already feel like we are making progress. This is harder than anything we have ever done. But I know if we get out of this mess, our family will be able to face anything. I also know that we can't do this without you." Tim wanted her to know he wanted to be there.

Ti started to talk, but Sophie interrupted her. "Grammy, we forgot to give you your present." Kyle was running up behind her.

"Boy, you kids only go one speed: fast," Ti said with a smile. "A present for me? How can that be in the budget?" She opened the envelope the two children had decorated and looked at the card. "Super Saver, eh?" she said with a wink. "I think you learned more than I thought last week. I am going to hang this on the fridge so I can see it every day. What do you think, Kyle and Sophie? Want to help me?"

The three of them went into the kitchen and Tricia looked at Tim. "What was that all about? I wasn't expecting her to react like that."

"Remember," Tim said, "we haven't been in her life for a while. Then we swoop in with two kids and a truckload of debt and expect her to behave like it is normal. That isn't fair." He started to laugh. Tricia joined in. "Do you think we expected too much of her? I can't believe she didn't just kick us out the door." As he spoke, Tim was looking through the door to the kitchen. He watched the three of them as they decided where to hang the card on the fridge, as if it was a masterpiece. He was beginning to realize that Ti could be looking for something more than just helping them with their financial problems.

Ti walked back into the living room after getting the kids back into their creative zone. She looked at Tricia and Tim and noticed that they were behaving differently. Last week, they barely looked at each other, and Tim spent most of the afternoon staring into space. They were now laughing, and Ti could feel the warmth between them. There was a difference.

"Well, are you ready to begin? We got off on the wrong foot, and I would like to get back on track. Congratulations, Tim, for selling that car. I know it wasn't easy and it wasn't something you wanted to do," Ti said, looking over at Tim.

"You know, at first I was angry about the car. All I could think of was how much I loved that car and how it wasn't fair. I hated the pair of you for making me sell my car. But once I made the deal, it felt great to make a difference for my family. A layoff makes you feel like you're failing your wife and kids. A part of me knew that I was contributing to our financial mess, but I couldn't get past me in all of it. It was so easy to let Trish take the fall for it. Selling that car made me realize I was wrong and I could do something about it. Weird, eh?" Tim ran his fingers through his hair and looked over at Tricia.

Tricia was a little taken aback by Tim's words. She hadn't even realized that it bothered him to be out of work. From her perspective, it was an extended vacation for him. It bothered her, but she had never said anything. "I never knew, Tim. I thought you were enjoying your time off. I didn't think you even cared about what was going on. It bothered me, but I thought it best to leave you alone. I wish we had talked back then."

Tim put his hand on Tricia's knee. "I am sorry, Trish. I shouldn't have let you do this alone. It was just easier to walk away from it all, and I promise I won't do that again."

Ti didn't know what to do. This was a big moment for the pair of them, and she didn't know whether to leave the room or not. She decided to lighten up the mood instead and get them back on track. They had plenty of time to deal with these personal issues later.

"Okay, okay, break it up. It is great that you are figuring out how to make your marriage better, but I'm an old lady. I don't have much time. Now, can we get back to your finances?" She looked over at the pair of them; they were smiling. "Well?"

"Sure," said Tricia. "We want to tell you about our week. We did well, considering we are new at this. The hardest part was calling the credit card companies. We were both nervous, but we did great."

"What happened?" asked Ti.

"In the first round of calls, the answer was 'no' or 'call back later.' Because I have missed payments, they said that I have to show them I can pay on time before they would look at reducing the rate. There was one company, though, that agreed to let us go to a lower-interest card. That gave us some hope. So we went for round two and asked for a supervisor. We did better this time and only had one card company that wouldn't change the rate at all. We have to pay on time for the next two months before they will consider lowering it."

"I knew that having the interest rate lowered would be a challenge because of your payment record. I am so proud of the two of you for not giving up. I thought it would take more than a couple of tries to get to where you are. You two are good," Ti said with a smile. "But don't give up on the other one. You want to keep pestering until you get the lowest rate possible."

"I thought we had done well, considering neither one of us knew what we were doing. I think persistence is the key, and I don't think Trish and I will stop until we get the fourth card lowered as well. We also came up with a repayment plan based on the rates. Would you like to see it?" Tim took the payment schedule out of the envelope.

Ti took the paperwork and looked at the figures. "Wow, I am impressed. This is a well-thought-out plan. I like the idea of paying off the smallest balance first, because it gives you a sense of accomplishment. You were also aware of the interest rate you were paying. So you're two for two."

"On the next page is our budget. We had an easy time of it. I can't believe all the money we were both wasting," Tim said.

"We had an easy time with everything but the food," Tricia

interjected. "I am finding staying within our food budget hard, Grammy Ti. I don't want to eat junk every day."

"Patricia, I know it's hard. If it was easy, no one would overspend. What you need to learn to do is buy what is on sale and be creative. In my generation, we didn't have a choice. There was no credit card to tide us over. We only had so much money and that was it. I can tell you it is cheaper to make food from scratch. It takes a little more time, but it is cheaper, tastes better, and is better for you. You are just going to have to deal with this. You're not going to go hungry on that budget. Do you know how many people do go hungry?" Ti was not going to let Tricia feel sorry for herself. She had plenty of money to provide decent meals. "When I was a child, we would have one big meal on Sunday. It was a chicken, a ham, or roast beef. Then, my mother would make that meat stretch three days. She made the best soup out of scraps."

"So that's where you get your talent from," Tim said with a smile. "But we are still falling behind by $400 a month. We worked hard at this and we don't know where else to cut back. We were over by $1,600. It's a big difference, but it's not enough. So, now what do we do?"

"Let's get some more coffee and then we will tackle the next stage. I think we need to take a moment and celebrate how far you have come in a week. I would like to celebrate theses baby steps before I make you run." Ti chuckled. "I have some freshly made scones in the kitchen. Interested?"

"You don't have to ask me twice," Tim said as he followed Ti out to the kitchen.

Lessons from Chapter 9

Cooking from Scratch

Many items are cheaper when you make them from scratch. It takes time and organization to cook from scratch, which is why people pay more for convenience foods. This is a major way to lower food expenses. Baking cookies from scratch is about a third of the cost of buying them, and you can have fun with your kids as well. If you bought a bread-maker during the craze, get it out of the cupboard. Or look for a used one on eBay or Craigslist. Homemade bread is about half the cost of store-bought, and you cannot beat the taste. On Sunday afternoon, bake cookies and make a few meals to freeze for midweek convenience. This step alone can lower your food bill significantly.

Clipping Coupons and Finding Bargains

We have lost the art of finding the deal, because our lives have gotten too busy. In the Depression, they had no choice. There was a finite amount of money, and they had to stretch it as far as possible to feed their family for a week. We need to go back to that era of buying what is on sale and clipping coupons for everything.

I remember in the '80s, clipping coupons was popular. There were books and magazine articles written about maximizing the benefits of coupon-clipping. You could even buy coupon wallets. What happened? If you put in the time and effort, you can lower the amount you pay for your groceries. You can even look online to find sites that provide coupons for almost anything.

Selling Stuff

It is simple: if you don't need it, sell it. There are so many avenues nowadays. You have eBay, Craigslist, consignment shops, and garage sales. There are swap shops and church bazaars. Start with the bigger items like a car and work down to the smaller items. Be brutal. When you get back on your feet, you can find out what you missed and start saving to replace it. Remember, the important question is whether you need it or not.

In the Depression, the average house was much smaller, and they did not have the closet and storage space like we do today. They could not hold on to as much excess because they did not have the room. Unneeded items were sold or traded for something that was needed. We need to adopt that way of living. Clear out that garage or closet! Happy selling.

Chapter 10 – Boosting Income to Balance the Budget

After getting fresh coffee and checking in with the kids, Ti, Tricia, and Tim gathered in the living room again. Tim got the rest of the paperwork out and passed it on to Ti. "As you can see, even with all of our hard work, we still don't have a balanced budget."

"The first part of every financial plan is to reduce expenses. You have done a great job. Now we have to look at increasing income. We have to make up that difference as well as pay down your debt and build up some savings. The only way to do that is to bring in more money. Patricia, I hate to be the bad guy, but you are going to have to work full time. Is that a possibility where you are now?"

"Let me get this straight: You want me to fire the housekeeper, cook from scratch, and go from part-time to full-time work. I think that is too much for anybody to take. There has to be another way." She was now pleading with her grandmother.

"Patricia, there is no other way. Tim is working a full week and there is no overtime right now. I want him to be creative and find some extra income as well, but you will have to move up to full time. You need to double your income, and I would like you, Tim, to see if you could make an extra $200 each month somehow. That will be for savings." She looked to Tim for support.

"I don't know about this. This is huge. Tricia working full time is a big change for our family. There are only so many hours in the day. How is she going to manage?"

"She is going to manage with your help. You two will make a schedule for the chores and household responsibilities with the kids. Your work schedules will control who does what when. You are in a partnership now. You don't get to sit around and watch anymore, Tim. Get the kids involved as well. It should never have been all of Patricia's responsibility anyway. My whole family worked when I was young. We did whatever we had to do to bring in money and to make sure we did all the chores. You have to start thinking like that."

The thought of working full time overwhelmed Tricia. She did like the thought of Tim helping out. He rarely did any of the chores around the house. He thought it was his job to work, keep the cars running, and take out the garbage. Having Tim taking part in the household would change a lot.

"Look, I will ask on Monday if there are any more hours. I can't promise anything. I never wanted any more hours than I had, so I am not sure how it works. I can manage only if Tim agrees to split the work at home. I can't do everything. What do you think, Tim?" Tricia didn't know what to expect from him. This was new territory for them.

"Well, I'm not sure. I didn't think you would have to go to work full time, but we are not in a position to argue about it. Let's see what your work says first. I guess I am going to have to help out more. When I was growing up, it was my mom who did all the housework. Look at my mom now. I guess if she can change, so can I. Don't expect perfection though." Tim smiled at Tricia. Then he looked over at Ti and asked, "How am I supposed to make an extra $200? There won't be overtime for at least six months."

"Ever hear of thinking outside the box, Tim? Take something you like to do and make money at it. You don't have your own car to work on and you loved to do that. Why not work on someone else's?"

Ti had always believed in making money doing what you love. That is why she took a job so far from home. She loved art, so she felt honored to clean the gallery downtown every morning before it opened. In the afternoon, before she caught the bus home, she would wander from piece to piece, wondering what the artist was trying to say to her. Each day, it was different and she enjoyed the experience.

"I never thought about working on cars for money. Let me think on it and see if I can come up with something. That would be great, because it wouldn't be work for me." The look on Tim's face changed from doubt to excitement. You could see the wheels turning. He was already making a list in his head of what he could do and what he would charge. He was thinking $200 may just be the start.

"I think that is enough for one day, don't you? You both have a big job ahead of you. Your finances will turn around if you can bring in that extra income. You will be reducing your debt and saving for your future. Won't that make you feel great?" Ti turned to the pair sitting on the couch and grinned. "You deserve a reward. Homemade soup, anyone?"

The conversation at the dining room table was full of cheer. The kids, excited about their masks, paraded around the table showing them off. Tricia teased Tim about his cooking skills and he joked about how hard full-time work was. Ti was unusually quiet. She was enjoying this time very much and she didn't want it to end. A week was a long time between visits, with the house so quiet. It had been ages since she had regular visitors. Her son used to visit every week until his money problems kept him away. Since his death, life had been quiet and lonely. She had felt God had answered her prayers when Patricia called her that day. She didn't know what she was going to do when she had solved their financial problems and they no longer needed her.

"What's wrong, Grammy Ti?" asked Sophie. "Why are you not talking?"

Everyone looked at Ti. "Well, Sophie, I was just listening. I enjoy listening to you talk at once. It reminds me when your grandpa was young. Could never keep him quiet or still," she continued as she looked over at Tricia. "He was a quite a character, wasn't he, Patricia?"

Patricia hadn't thought much about her father in the past couple of years. When her mother had left, she pushed both of her parents out of her mind because it was just too painful. Looking back, she did remember her father being energetic and he was always going from one project to the next. He rarely finished anything. He always made her laugh, though. "Yes. He was a character. And as you can see, his namesake is one as well." Both she and Ti laughed at Kyle dancing like an African warrior wearing his mask.

After lunch, everyone worked together to clean up lunch dishes and the children's craft table. Ti helped Kyle and Sophie wrap their masks in tissue paper to protect them on the way home. They said good-bye with the promise to return the following week.

On the drive home, Tricia thought about the task ahead of her. She did not know about working extra hours. It seemed her days were already full. It just all seemed so hard. Even if she did what her grandmother suggested, it would be years before they were back on track. She wasn't sure if she could last, working this hard and living this poor for that long. She hadn't been brought up like that. She just worked on her parents until she got what she wanted. It was very easy. She wanted that life back.

"What are you thinking about?" Tim asked.

"I wish I could go back. I wish I would have understood how good I had it. I just wanted more and more. That is exactly how I was, growing up. I would get my parents to buy me the latest fad and then, a week later, I was asking for something else. I always got what I wanted, but I was never satisfied." Tricia looked out the window.

"Maybe there is a lesson in all of this, Trish. We were both wanting more and not appreciating what we had. I got everything I wanted until boredom set in and I'd want something else. I didn't enjoy anything for long, except my car," Tim chuckled. "But even that was temporary. I had already been looking for a better car. I was planning on buying one as soon as I got overtime again."

"You never told me that. I thought you loved this car." Tricia looked over at him in surprise.

"I did. But I had finished all the work and I was looking for a new challenge. Now that I have to sell it, I value it so much more. I feel like I have woken up from some long sleep. I wasn't living. Everything was fun for a while and then I just felt numb."

Tricia thought over what Tim had said. She realized that she too had felt that shopping brought her happiness. The feeling never lasted. That is why she kept shopping. She didn't get what it all meant, but she knew that it had to change. She wanted to be happy without having to buy something new each week. Lost in thought, neither realized how much they had learned on the short drive home.

Lessons from Chapter 10

Do What You Have To

You need to work as long and as hard as you can to bring in the money you need to balance the budget. Everyone needs to be working on it. Kids can do paper routes, babysit, or do yard work for someone. Take on a second job or do small jobs on the side for people in your area. If you find something you love to do, it makes it much easier. Take your hobby and make money at it. In the Depression, there were people who sold scraps they had found going through the garbage. There is no shame in doing whatever you have to, to provide for your family.

Money Doesn't Buy Happiness

It is that simple. Most people I know who grew up during the Depression talk of hard times that still had many moments of happiness. They didn't have much, but they enjoyed life anyway. Money can make you feel more secure, but it does not guarantee happiness—nor do the items money can buy. You have the power to choose happiness, regardless of your circumstances.

It is difficult to be happy when you do not know how you are going to pay your rent or mortgage. It is difficult to be happy when bill collectors are calling you. Even so, it can be done. You can choose to have fun with your kids today. The bill collectors do not dictate your mood; you do. Consciously choose activities that are fun and make you happy. Do not put off happiness until the mortgage is paid. What a waste of life. There is no guarantee for tomorrow, so stay in the present moment and enjoy today.

Chapter 11 – Make Money Doing What You Love

On Sunday, Tricia stayed in bed all day. She just couldn't face the fact she had to work full time. She hated her work as a receptionist, and working at it for twenty-five hours each week was enough for her. The only reason she had taken the job was because it had fit into her schedule. She just put in her hours at her desk and left. She rarely attended any office functions and could only name a few of her co-workers. It never dawned on her before that she hated her job. The thought of being there every day was unbearable.

Tim checked in on her every once in a while and told the kids to stay quiet because Mom wasn't feeling well. There had been many days in the past few months that Tricia hadn't been well. Tim had begun to worry there was something seriously wrong with her, but now he understood what was making her feel so ill. He figured that since they had started working on their financial plan, she would feel better. It surprised him that she was feeling down again today.

He went into the bedroom quietly and sat on the side of the bed. "What's wrong, Trish?"

"I'm fine, Tim. I just have a headache." Tricia turned away from him.

"We both know that is not true. I have let you handle life too long on your own. I am here now. So, what is wrong?" Tim insisted. He wanted to let her know he wasn't going away.

Tricia debated whether to tell him or not. They were never good at discussing their personal feelings. All these years together and they didn't get past the surface. She decided she would give him a chance. "I hate my job, and the thought of spending forty hours a week there gives me a stomachache. I know I am supposed to be strong and be an adult and fix this, but I hate that job. I was just doing it because the hours were right for our family."

"How long have you hated that job? You never complained to me." Tim was in shock.

"Since the day I started. I stuck with it for the pay and the hours. But Lord help me, I can't work there any more than I already do."

"Wow! I can't believe we never talked about this. You've hated your job for the past six years, and I never even knew. There is something wrong here, Trish. I should have known." Tim sat there shaking his head, looking dazed. "Six years," he repeated.

"You know, Tim, all you ever asked about when you came home was how the kids were doing and when supper would be ready. I didn't tell you because I thought you didn't care. I didn't tell you because I thought it didn't matter to you. I did what I had to do and stayed quiet doing it."

"Trish, everything about you matters to me. We can't live apart emotionally and expect to get through this. What is happening to us is a wake-up call. I am so sorry that I didn't pay more attention. I just took it for granted that you liked your job. What else don't I know about you?" Tim asked.

"I am allergic to daisies," Tricia replied with a smirk.

"I thought those were your favorite flowers. I always wondered why you put them in the front window of the living room, since you never go in there. When I asked you about it, you said it was because the flowers made the room look so pretty. I can't believe you never said you were allergic to them. That is going to stop. We need to start being honest with each other. What flowers *do* you like?"

"I never told you about the daisies because it was one of few sweet things you did just for me. I thought if I complained, you would stop. Honestly, my favorite is yellow roses. Also, I hate that perfume you buy me every year for Christmas. Perhaps we should play the dating game and find out what else we don't know about each other." Tricia started to laugh.

"You must love me to have put up with that all these years. Changing flowers and perfume is easy enough. A job is a little different. What are you going to do?"

"I'll ask my boss tomorrow about what options I have. I don't know if there is any chance of increasing my hours." Tricia's face saddened.

"Remember what Ti said about finding something you love and making money at it? What would you love to do?"

"I don't know Tim. I only remember looking forward to shopping. I am a bland person. I am not good at anything and I never had many hobbies."

"Trish, you are a good mom and a great wife. You have made a beautiful home here. You make great meals and the place is always sparkling. With two kids and a slob for a husband, that takes talent," he said, poking her. "You could get a job as a professional shopper. What if some millionaire needed help spending his money? Let's get on the computer and look up shopping on the employment site and see what comes up. You game?"

"I'll go with you, just to get you to leave me alone. It might be interesting to see what is available out there. Let's go."

Tricia and Tim went to the computer desk. The remnants of their card-making project were all over the place. Tricia laughed, remembering that day. It was fun. They needed to have another family project to work on.

"There are several categories under shopping. Most of the jobs have to do with working at stores. Here's one that may interest you. There is a department store looking for someone in the purchasing department. What about that, Trish?"

"Did you not read that they need someone with experience? I have no experience." Tricia looked glum.

"You have had a lifetime of experience. Apply for it and see what happens. If you don't get this job, you may find out how to get the next one. What's the worst that can happen?"

"They will look at me like I have four heads." Tricia giggled. She just couldn't help herself. "Then they may lock me up because they think I am insane to apply."

Tricia never even thought of looking for a different job. She did not realize there were so many different kinds of positions available. After checking out some more job sites, she found three or four that interested her. Tim helped her work on her résumé and she applied for a few positions online.

"Well, now it is time to wait and see. I know you will find something you like. You never know, this financial crisis may turn out to be the best thing that ever happened to you. I don't want you going through life hating what you're doing just because you think your family needs you to. Life's too short to be unhappy, Trish. Let's make a pact that we will do what is right by our family, but we will always try to do it in a manner that makes us happy. Are you in?" Tim grabbed her by the hand.

"You know, I didn't realize how much I put my own happiness aside. I think that is why I shopped so much. It made me feel good. The rest of it just left me feeling sad. I think I had given up on life. Now I just want to feel good again and I want us to be happy. Let's go get the kids and do something together. After we have put them to bed, we'll check and see if there are any replies to my applications."

There were no responses later that evening, but that didn't worry Tricia and Tim. It was Sunday night and they didn't expect anyone to receive her résumé until the morning. It was exciting thinking about a new job. Tricia thought about the different positions she had applied for. She knew she would enjoy working at any of them. They involved fashion and purchasing, and she had a lifetime of experience in both these areas. It was a nice change to be excited.

Lessons from Chapter 11

Make Money Doing What You Love

Parents often advise their children to get a good-paying job with benefits. It doesn't matter what the position is. It just needs to be secure. That is because parents want their children to grow up to be financially secure. This perpetuates the idea that money comes before happiness. This is wrong.

Think about the last time you went to a store or a restaurant and you met someone who clearly loved his or her job. For example, you notice a waitress in a coffee shop you go to every morning. She is cheerful and efficient. She makes you feel like you are the most important person in the room. Each day, you want to sit in her section. So does everyone else. The manager recognizes this and gives her more hours. She also makes more tips than any of the other waitresses. The manager puts her in charge of the day shift. In the years that follow, she saves her money and becomes part owner. It is a thriving business today. Her success is because she loved her job, did it well, and had a plan for the future.

Now think about being in a job you hate. Do you go above and beyond what is expected? Are you pleasant to work with? Do you do the best work possible? Is there someone offering you a raise to keep you? Can you see how this can work against you in the long term?

Those who have been successful in life have found something they loved and worked at it until they were the best they could be. Often this came with financial rewards as well. Can you imagine being paid for a job you would do for free?

If you are not in the situation where you can leave a job you hate, start building a career on the side doing something you love. The possibilities are endless. Computers, photography, music, baking, sewing, talking on the phone, reading about celebrities, and writing are all areas where people have started as a hobby and are now making money and having fun.

Don't Believe the Economy is Too Bad to Find Work

If you are in the position that you need money now and do not have the luxury of holding out for something you love, know there are jobs out there. The area of demand may change, but there is always opportunity. You may have to change your profession. You may have to work two jobs instead of one. You may have to create your own opportunity. If you have handed out one hundred résumés with no job offers, don't stop looking. It just may be the next résumé you hand out will lead you to the right position. Someone, somewhere, needs you. You only need to believe that.

In the Depression, when there was a 25 percent unemployment rate (and this was a time when few women worked), people got creative and did what they had to. Think outside the box and do what others are not doing and you will find a way to make it. Look for businesses that would thrive in a recession. I just heard a story of a woman who got a job in a company that recovers cable equipment from homes of past subscribers. I would have never thought about that area of business.

There are other strategies to use when looking for a job. You could volunteer until a position becomes available. Every month, you could visit a list of businesses you wish to work for, to keep yourself top of mind. You could come up with a creative business proposal for your own business and apply for government funding. Businesses may be interested in trading your work for their services. Turn your hobby into cash. Whatever you do, do not give up. If you are positive, active, and think outside the box, you will get work.

Chapter 12 – Once You Commit to Change, Change Will Happen

In the morning, Tricia called her boss at work to talk about increasing her hours. She was just going through the motions. She now knew this was not where she wanted to work. Her boss explained that her position may be eliminated because of the reduced workload. Now, instead of looking at increased hours, she may be out of a job. She had no choice but to pursue another career.

After she hung up, she went online to see if there had been any responses to the applications she had sent the previous night. She saw she had two messages. The first let her know they did not feel she had the experience to be the head of purchasing in their company. The second message asked her to call to arrange an interview with their human resources department. It was also in purchasing, but it was a junior position. She dialed the number and she felt shaky when she asked for the extension. She knew first impressions, even on the phone, mattered and she wanted to sound confident. Luckily, she only had to speak to a receptionist who arranged an interview time.

Tricia had never interviewed for a job before. For her current position, the previous hire was a friend who moved to another city, and the job was handed to Tricia. Because of her inexperience with interviews, she knew that she needed any help she could get. She decided she would search online for tips on how to have a successful interview.

The information that Tricia found offered common interview questions so she could prepare suitable answers. She also read some questions that she could ask at an interview. She felt prepared when the phone rang that afternoon at the pre-arranged time. When the interview was over, the interviewer asked to meet Tricia in person the next day. Although nervous, she looked forward to the meeting. She somehow knew she was on the right track. It just felt right.

When Tim came home from work, Tricia couldn't wait to tell him everything. She was so excited about the interview that she almost forgot to tell him what her boss had said. Only the month before, she would have been devastated that they were thinking of letting her go, and today, she almost forgot about it. Her world was changing so quickly.

At first, Tim looked worried about her current position and then showed excitement about the new possibilities. "You know, Trish, you said out loud you didn't like your job. Now, twenty-four hours later, you are looking at changing your career, whether you want to or not. My mom used to say 'God works in mysterious ways,' and I think she is right. I think we have to come to the realization that we need to change and then God helps us. Every step we have taken in the last month has been like that. We see something is wrong, and then help just happens to come along. Can you see that or am I losing my mind?" Tim turned to Tricia to see her reaction.

"I have seen it too, Tim. For the last several months, I've been getting these anxiety attacks when it just gets to be too much. Just when I think I am going down for the count, money shows up or the gas bill is less or the kids do something remarkable. I begged God for help and I thought he was ignoring me. I think I was wrong. He was helping me, but not in the way I thought he should. It is hard to see any good when you are as low as I was. I also thought you didn't care. I had nobody to turn to. I hated my job, I was broke, and I felt sick to my soul. There was no light at the end of the tunnel for me. Now I can see there was a reason I went through all of this. I am changing my life for the better because it got so bad. Or it got so bad so I would change my life. I am not sure which."

"I didn't realize it was that bad for you, Trish. I am sorry you felt alone and that I didn't care. I do care, Tricia. I want us to be happy together. I don't want to be poor, so I am going to do my part to get us out of here. You are not alone anymore. I can see our lives getting better because of all of this. I already feel closer to you, and I love hanging out with you and the kids. I am also excited about working on cars. I talked to the guys at work, and they thought it was a great idea. They would rather pay me $20 an hour than a mechanic $100. I am already booked on Friday to change some spark plugs for a guy. I figure I will make about $60. I honestly think I can make more than $200 extra a month."

"That is great, Tim. But before you get too busy, we need to make up a schedule for the kids. I know we can work it out. I am so glad that you are happy doing this. It makes it so much easier for me because I don't feel so guilty."

"No need to feel guilty, Trish. We did this together and we will fix it together. I don't blame you anymore. I know I was a fool. But I think it can work out. I would much rather work on cars for money than do overtime at the plant, so something good came out of it already. Let's get you ready for that interview tomorrow. Have you researched the company yet?"

They both turned to the computer and compiled all the information Tricia felt she needed for the next day. Tim pretended he was the interviewer and put her through a mock interview. Tricia became comfortable answering the questions. She was confident that this was the area she wanted to get into and she believed she had the experience to back her up. She had done everything she could to prepare. The rest was up to the company.

Lesson from Chapter 12

Hard Work Never Hurt Anyone

If you lived through the Depression, you know what hard work is. Whether you were five years old or fifty years old, you worked from sunup to sundown to do whatever was necessary to keep the family going. If you talk to someone of that era, they do not complain about it. That was just the way it was.

For many of us who were not alive then, we do not know the meaning of hard work. We have so many conveniences today that even daily tasks are much easier. We have unions and labor laws to protect us from working too many hours or in dangerous conditions. The lesson to learn from the current economic crisis is to commit to doing what is necessary to protect your family, and help will come. Hard work will pay off. When you are telling stories about this era to your grandchildren, you will not complain; that was just the way it was.

Chapter 13 – Breaking Old Habits

The next morning, Tricia rushed to get ready. She was so excited, she was having a difficult time remaining calm. She did not want the sales manager to mistake excitement for nerves. She dropped Tim and the kids off and made her way to the appointment. She couldn't believe how giddy she felt. She did not think it was possible to ever feel excited or happy again.

Tricia was confident during the interview and felt she had answered the questions well. The sales manager told her that they had ten candidates for the job and they hoped to narrow it to three for the final set of interviews. These would occur in front of a panel of several management team members and the head of purchasing. She would know how she fared in the next couple of days.

On the drive home, Tricia thought about going to the mall. She would normally celebrate her great interview by buying a treat for herself and for the kids. It would feel very good to buy something new in honor of the occasion. She pulled into the parking lot and found a spot right in front of her favorite store. She wanted to buy an outfit for the second interview. She was just about to get out of the car when it hit her—she couldn't go shopping.

At first, she was angry. It didn't seem fair that she couldn't celebrate or make sure she had the most suitable outfit to wear. Then she started to think about all the progress they had made. A new sweater wasn't a guarantee for success, but it would make her feel great. She debated back and forth for a few minutes before deciding to go home. It wasn't easy.

Anger erased the excitement of the successful interview. For the first time since she had met with her grandmother, she felt the weight of the sacrifices she would have to make to clear up their debt. On paper, it had seemed very easy. Faced with the reality of today, Tricia realized there were going to be times when it would be tough. She again felt the weight of her life. Just when she thought everything was under control, a new wave of anxiety swept over her. Why couldn't this all go away?

By the time she had reached her house, she had come to terms with her decision, but she had not regained her jovial mood. When she walked in the door, she looked defeated. Tim came over to her, concerned with her demeanor. He had assumed the interview had not gone well. "Was it that bad, Trish? I thought you would have aced that interview."

"The interview was fine," Tricia said, her voice lacking enthusiasm.

"Why aren't you ecstatic then? What happened?" Tim asked with concern.

"I did great in the interview and I was excited. I decided to go shopping and celebrate and buy something for the final interview. Then I realized I couldn't go shopping. I may never be able to drop by the mall on the spur of the moment and buy something ever again."

"Oh, Trish, I know it is hard. I know that it seems like forever before we have money again. It won't be. Ti never said this would be easy. We are both going to have times when we think we can't do it. That's why we have to work as a team. We need to keep each other going. We can do this, and one day we will be able to buy whatever we want with cash. Let's go shopping in your closet for something to wear. It would be fun to watch you try on different outfits and maybe a piece of lingerie or two."

Tim grabbed Tricia and hugged her as he laughed. Tricia didn't want to laugh, but she couldn't help herself. They both knew she didn't have much lingerie to model. Tricia thought it might be fun to try on outfits. She tried to remember exactly what she had up there.

"You could do a fashion show for the kids and me, and we will pick out our favorite. Then, after they go to bed, I get to pick my personal favorite. What do you think?" Tim was trying to get Tricia to agree.

Tricia smiled at him. She couldn't believe that Tim would think of doing a fashion show. That was not like him at all. "I'll try it. It could be fun. I am not even sure what I have up there. I hope the perfect outfit is sitting there waiting for me. Let's go get the kids and we will do it before supper."

Tricia enjoyed trying on the clothes. She hadn't cared about how she looked at work, so much of her work apparel looked new. She found the perfect suit in a charcoal gray that she had only worn once. She looked professional yet fashionable and thought it would be the right look for someone in the purchasing department. Sophie was also trying on clothes, and Kyle and Tim were getting a kick out of her trying to walk in high heels.

After dinner, the four of them played cards. Then Tim and Tricia worked together to get the kids bathed, read to, and in bed. It was usually Tricia's job, and she found it was much easier with the two of them.

Later, in the den, Tricia told Tim, "It was so much fun tonight as a family. Usually bedtime is stressful, but you helped and I actually enjoyed it. This is how it should be every night."

"I didn't know how much work it was to get the two of them to bed. I have to say, I am impressed you did it on your own and I am sorry I haven't helped that much before. You have to work on my caveman side," Tim teased Tricia. "So, are you feeling better?"

"You know, at the mall I felt devastated. I thought that I couldn't go through with this. You again helped me. I wish we had gotten to this point a few years ago so our lives didn't get so out of control." Tricia slumped on the couch and looked defeated again.

"Trish, we can't change the past; let it go. I was wrong and you were wrong. That life is over. We have both changed for the better. Our marriage has changed for the better. The kids are happier than I ever remember. Is going through this change such a bad thing? You know, I was talking to the guys at work about this, and everyone is living their own version of it. None of them know how to manage money either. I have become somewhat of a celebrity there, sharing Ti's advice. Everyone wants to know what to do next because they are as lost as we are. But there have been some tragedies. Bill and his wife broke up months ago, and it was because of money. They couldn't work together and they couldn't stop blaming each other. We can make this a success, not a tragedy. I want that. Do you?"

"Of course I do. I am a little ashamed of myself. I was so down about not buying something new, even though I have a closet full of clothes. I don't think I have been grateful for anything. Tonight, I thought about all the clothes I haven't worn yet. I have spent my life whining about what I didn't have, instead of enjoying what I did. I don't want to be like that anymore."

"I know what you are saying, Trish. I am so happy that we have had this opportunity to reflect on what matters and how lucky we are. We're broke ... so what? Look at our kids and how much fun we had as a family tonight. We didn't do that when I was working every hour of overtime I could get. All we need to do is to focus on being grateful. We need to break the habit of *want* because that is all it is. A nasty habit," Tim said with a smile.

"You are right, Tim. I am ready to break that habit once and for all."

Both Tim and Tricia sat in silence, feeling the sense of gratitude that had eluded them for so many years. They both knew that even though their circumstances hadn't changed, their outlook on life had. It felt like the beginning of a new life.

Lessons from Chapter 13

Breaking Old Habits

Experts say it takes twenty-one days to break a habit. Think about the habits you have created that are sabotaging your financial stability. Once you have identified them, come up with an action plan for the next twenty-one days to eliminate them. For instance, if you go to Tim Horton's or Starbucks every day, set up your coffeemaker on timer so fresh coffee is available to you every morning. Eventually, you will not even think about stopping on your way to work. Once you break the habit, Starbucks can be a monthly treat, not a daily habit.

Family First

Whenever you are deciding to make a purchase, calculate how many hours you need to work to pay for it. Knowing the time you will miss with your family will help put this purchase into perspective. There are thousands of children who would trade in their toys and electronics to have one-on-one time with one or both of their parents. When you put your family first, the family dynamics will change for the better.

Chapter 14 – Ask for Help

Tricia had waited anxiously for word on the interview. She knew that she had done the best job she could, and it was difficult leaving her future in the hands of others. She not only needed this job, she desperately *wanted* this job. Tricia had never known what it was like to want to go to work every morning. She had not felt excited about work for so long, and she was having a hard time containing her emotions.

Every time the phone rang, she jumped. She was glad that this was not a day she had to go to the office, because she was sure they would know what was going on. She did not want to let work know she was applying elsewhere until she had something solid. If they let her go before she had another position, their finances would take a turn for the worse.

By mid-afternoon, she had given up and decided that she would go online and look for other positions. She now knew she had to change careers, so she might as well take it seriously. She looked for anything that would make the money she needed, as well as be something she would enjoy doing.

When the phone call she had been waiting for finally did come, she had almost forgotten about the potential interview. She had posted her résumé at a new job Web site and looked at a few opportunities she thought might be a good fit. When she answered, she was a little distracted, so it surprised her that it was the call. She was in the final three. When she hung up, she started dancing and yelling. She felt her life had taken the turn she was waiting for. Finally, she could enjoy some good news and she felt grateful.

When Tim came home, she jumped in his arms and started whooping and hollering. The kids were following him and were at first frightened by their crazy mother. As it became clear that this was a celebration, the kids joined in and started yelling as well. It took Tim several minutes to settle the group down.

"What did they say? When do you have to go back? Did they give you any clue of how you fit in the final three?" Tim wanted some details before he got too excited.

"You know, I didn't ask any questions. I was just so excited, I got the time and date of my interview, thanked them, and hung up. I know this is my job, Tim. It feels too right not to be. It is everything I could want in a job, and the pay is enough to meet the budget. What could be better?" Tricia was grinning from ear to ear.

"Let's celebrate," Tim said. "Root beer floats for everybody."

The kids sang and danced their way into the kitchen, and Tim went to the refrigerator to get the ingredients. As they sat around the table and enjoyed the treat, Tim turned to Tricia and smiled. "Who'd have guessed it, Trish? Six months ago, we were headed for disaster, and look at the turnaround. We still are not the Trumps, but we are going to make it. We are going to keep our house, which I thought was impossible. We are happier broke than we ever were when we thought we were rich. What a difference time and a plan makes. I wished we had visited your grandmother years ago. I can see we were lucky to have no other choice but to call her. She has helped us both emotionally and financially, and we have a new family member. Isn't this great?"

"I haven't got the job yet, so don't get too excited," Tricia laughed. "But I know what you mean. I was getting to the point where I was wondering if life was worth it. Why bother getting out of bed to do battle in a war you are losing? I had no hope of fixing anything, let alone enjoying life again. I thought if I just kept sweeping it under the rug, it would go away. Unfortunately, the problem just kept getting bigger and bigger until I couldn't deal with it. We are so lucky that Grammy Ti helped us. I don't know what I would have done without her."

"I was thinking about that last night, Trish. Where do people go with problems like this? I went online and I found many places with information on budgeting, but it was confusing. There were spreadsheets and budget outlines, but no real advice on how to begin. There was no one to talk to. And of course, they don't serve homemade soup. Even if there was someone to talk to, it is humiliating showing how badly you have screwed up. It was horrible showing Ti our finances. After talking with the guys at work, I realized that so many people are where we are. You're in a place where you know you are in trouble, with no idea of how to get help. Then you find out what you have to do, like sell your favorite car, and it isn't easy following through."

"I know, Tim. I still get moments when I panic and I think I can't do this. I still sometimes have trouble looking past tomorrow without feeling overwhelmed. But I don't dread the future anymore. I am almost relieved that someone stopped me from shopping myself into bankruptcy. Well, not when I was at the mall the other day." Tricia smirked at Tim. "I can't wait until we see Grammy Ti again. I am excited to let her know what we have been doing and how well the job search is going. I hope I will be lucky enough to tell her I have the job by Saturday. And you already have some extra work lined up as well. Wait a minute. Do you have to work on that car Friday?" Tricia looked at Tim.

"Yeah, I do. Why?"

"That's when I have my interview. What are we going to do about the kids? You're going to have to change the time with your buddy."

"I can't. He is leaving on Saturday for Florida. He needs the work done on his car before then. I can't do it tomorrow night because you're working late. If I cancel, it will be harder getting jobs from any of the other guys at work. You know how they talk. What are we going to do?"

"I will have to call around for a babysitter. I am sure we can work it out. If you start dinner, I will do the calling," Tricia said.

"I knew the push into cooking was coming. I may as well just do it, eh?" Tim winked at Tricia and got up to begin dinner.

Tricia went to the den to find the list of babysitters. It surprised her that Tim started dinner without a fuss. She had expected him to balk at the idea, but he had agreed. They were making progress. She found the list and began making some calls. Not having much luck in finding one, Tricia began to panic. She went back to the kitchen to let Tim know.

"Well, we're in trouble. I can't find anyone available on Friday. What now?"

Tim turned from the stove. "Why don't we ask your grandmother? I have a feeling she would be happy to have them. She seems lonely and she also wants us to succeed. Call her."

"I don't know, Tim. Haven't we asked enough of her?" "I think she would love to do it. Call her."

Tim went back to cooking dinner, and Tricia went to the den and sat down by the phone. She wasn't sure that Tim was right. She did know the kids would love spending time with Grammy Ti. She decided it would do no harm to ask.

As she walked back into the kitchen, Tricia could smell something remarkable. "You were right again, Tim. She was happy to have them, especially since I had a job interview and you were working extra hours. I think I made her day. She wants to keep them overnight, and we can pick them up at our weekly Saturday visit. What are you making?" Tricia walked over to the stove.

"Omelets. I just took out everything I could find in the fridge and threw it in. Are you ready to eat?"

"I am starving. Kids, are you ready to eat?"

The kids helped Tricia set the table and they sat down to enjoy their omelets. Tricia commented on how great they were. The kids enjoyed them as well. She thought it would be a good idea to let Tim cook more often. They all cleaned up together after dinner, and Tim helped her get the kids to bed.

"It is practice time, Trish. Let's go through the interview again."

"I am nervous, Tim. I want this so bad. I feel like nothing ever works out for me, so I don't want to get too excited about this."

"Trish, it is not about this one interview. It is about you going after a job that can make enough income for our family, but also one that you will be happy doing. You have been miserable long enough. If you don't get this job, you will learn what you need to get the next one. There is never a 'do-or-die' moment in our lives. You get too stressed out thinking there is."

"That is easy for you to say. You got the job you wanted without even trying. You've enjoyed your time off during the shutdown, and you have never worried about anything," Tricia responded without even thinking. She hadn't even realized that she was still looking at Tim as having "the good life" while she struggled. "You just don't know what it's like."

"Is that what you think? You think I just got my dream job and lived happily ever after? Do you think that when I was a small boy, I dreamed of working in a cardboard factory?" He could not believe that Tricia would even think that.

"It just seems as if you never have any worries and you are always happy." Tricia was trying not to be bitter, but it was hard.

"Trish, I have as many worries as you. I just don't talk about them all the time. I fix what I can and let go of what I can't. Sometimes I think you prefer to be down about everything. I want you to know something. It nearly killed me to be on layoff. I went out and hung out with my friends because I didn't know what else to do. I felt if I stayed out of your way and didn't let you know how worried I was, then I was doing my job."

"Didn't you realize that I needed you here? I needed you to tell me we were going to be fine. I wanted you to figure out we were having money problems and I wanted you to help with the finances. You left me with too much. You may have been able to cope, but you left the rest of us on our own. It was terrible for me." Tricia started to cry and then stood up and turned toward Tim. "I am not going to cry anymore. The past is the past. You need to know that I can't do this alone. I will not be afraid to tell you how I feel again. I am worried about the interview Friday, so I need you to help me stay calm and focused. I need you to take care of the household and the kids tomorrow. I want to be able to concentrate on getting this position. We cannot go back to the way it was. Do we agree on that?"

Tim walked over to Tricia. "I know we still have some stuff to go through. When I try to hide from it, you need to give me a yank. And you need to stop being so negative. Look at the good that is happening instead of looking at the bad. It sometimes gets annoying being around you. I am not trying to hurt your feelings. It's just the way it is."

Tricia thought for a moment. She wanted to tell Tim that she wasn't a negative person, but she realized he was right. She used to be so happy and carefree. As long as she had a roof over her head and enough money to go shopping, she was happy. When did life start being such a struggle? "I didn't realize that I had gotten so bad. I have been so angry about everything for the past few years," Tricia admitted.

"What helps me the most is to be grateful. I look at you and the kids and I just feel so lucky. We have two great kids, and I still look forward to seeing you when I get home every day. Do you know how many lonely rich people there are out there?" Tim asked.

"I know, Tim. I am selfish. I want it all. I want a great family and a huge bank account."

"So, we start here with the great family and work toward the bank account. We can do it, you know. We have another chance. Now, are you ready to practice for your interview?"

Tricia felt better after going over the interview questions with Tim. She remembered her dad always saying "practice makes perfect" when she was studying for spelling. Spelling was her challenge in life, and her father was always the one to help her. He would make her go over her spelling list until she got all the words right. Tim was trying to do the same for her, and she realized she was lucky. Whenever she was in need of help, someone was there. She wasn't alone.

The next day at work, Tricia made it a point to be aware of what was going on around her. She had decided that—liking the job or not—she had to do her best. This was the first time in a long time that she tried to focus on her job performance. She tried to be friendlier with her co-workers and the customers. When she had some spare time, she went to help someone file instead of spending hours surfing the Internet. She did not realize how much more she enjoyed the job when she was trying to do it well.

When she got home, Tim had dinner waiting, and they enjoyed some time with the kids. Tricia could not remember a time when she came home to a prepared dinner. If Tim was in charge, he normally got take-out. Tonight, they enjoyed pasta and fresh bread.

"I pulled out the old bread-maker," Tim said proudly. "It was so easy and this bread is to die for. Why haven't we been using this?"

Tricia started to laugh. Tim talking about bread-makers would be the same as her talking about cars. It was unbelievable to see how much Tim had changed. Tricia thought back to the days when she was afraid to tell Tim about their finances. She thought about how unhappy and alone she felt. Here they were, just as broke, but now she felt that Tim was finally her partner.

On Friday morning, Tricia was nervous. She had a hard time concentrating on getting the kids ready for school. She realized that she hadn't packed their lunches when they were ready to go out the door. She took a deep breath and remembered what Tim had said about how no moment defines the rest of your life. She calmed down and thought about what was ahead. She knew that she was as prepared as she possibly could be for the interview. She also knew the job was in the field where she wanted to work. She decided that if this didn't work out today, there would be a better job around the corner.

The interview went well; Tricia felt proud of herself when she left the building. She had done her best in the interview, and she would know on Monday if that was enough. The interview took longer than expected, and she was late coming home. At least she didn't have to worry; the kids were with Grammy Ti. She wondered what the three of them would be doing tonight.

When Tricia walked into the house, she couldn't believe what she saw. The dining room table was set, and a vase of yellow roses sat on the middle of it. Tim was busy cooking something on the stove. She walked over and kissed him on the back of the neck.

"What's going on?"

Tim looked over at her. "Well, how did it go?"

"I think it went well," Tricia replied as she peeked into the pan. "I will know on Monday. What are you making?"

"It's only Hamburger Helper. I bought a bottle of wine that may make up for the food. Would you like a glass?"

"I would love one. So, how did the spark plug job go? Are they all set to go to Florida tomorrow?"

"You know, Trish, it was fun. I would have done it for nothing, but as you can see, I have sixty dollars over there on the counter. We were talking about it today, and another guy wants me to look at his exhaust. I told him I would check and see what day I was available to come over and I would let him know tomorrow. It will probably take four or five hours, and I'll charge $25 an hour. He thought that was a great deal because the garage told him it would be $150 just to look at it. I think I might be able to make more than $200 a month. I am pumped."

"That is great, Tim. The best part is that you are happy doing it. I just want to make sure that we stick to our strict budget, even when more money comes in. It has been a long time since we had more coming in than was going out. I don't want to blow this."

"We won't. We have Ti to make sure that doesn't happen. I wonder how she is doing with the kids. She was excited to see them, and she told me that she had some great surprises planned for them. They may not want to come home with us tomorrow."

"This wine is good, but I am starving. Is dinner ready yet?"

They sat down to a candlelight dinner and talked about what a treat it was to have dinner alone. After dinner, they decided to watch a movie from their collection of DVDs. They laughed about how few movies they owned that did not star a cartoon character. They decided on *Casablanca*. Watching an old movie made it seem like a real date, and they both enjoyed the evening. It was just one more example of how good life had become.

Lessons from Chapter 14

Ask for Help

When in a crisis, you need to reach out for help. If you are overwhelmed, it means the problem is too big for you to solve alone. Put your pride aside, decide what help you need and then ask for it. Don't expect those around you to guess that you are in trouble. Also, don't expect them to know how to help.

Get your family involved. Tell each member what you need from them. Have a schedule of household chores set up. Let them know about the budget and how they can help. Be honest when you cannot do it alone.

Look for professional help, if you feel you need it. There are different agencies out there set up to help in various ways. There is also information available to you on the Internet.

You Are Not Alone

We often feel alone when we are in trouble, especially if we blame ourselves. You are not alone. You are surrounded with people who love you, whether you know it or not. You also have God (or whatever higher power you believe in). Know there are people who care about you. Know that you are not alone.

Chapter 15 – Have Faith

On Saturday morning, Tricia and Tim headed off to her grandmother's. They talked about the wonderful breakfast they enjoyed alone. Tricia had felt like she had gone on vacation. She was looking forward to seeing her grandmother and the kids, but she was almost sad that her date with Tim had to end.

Both kids were watching for them out of the front window. When Tricia saw them grinning from ear to ear, she knew it was right not to worry about them. They looked as happy as she felt. It was good feeling, knowing that her family was happy as well.

When they were all settled in her grandmother's living room, the kids paraded their artwork and then put on a short play that they had worked on the previous evening. Ti, dressed as a pirate, looked ten years younger than she had last week. You could see the twinkle in her eye when she looked at the kids. Tricia still couldn't believe what a difference these few weeks had made.

"Well, kids, we have had our fun, but I need to talk to Mommy and Daddy now. You two work on that book we started, and we will break for lunch in a little while," Grammy Ti said. She turned to Tim and Tricia. "How did you two do this week? Do you have any news for me?"

"This was a good week all around, Grammy Ti. I finally realized that I was miserable at my job. When I called about extra hours, they told me they were thinking about letting me go because work had slowed down so much. I was surprised and relieved. It was killing me to think about working there full time."

"I had a feeling you were unhappy, Patricia. No matter how hard we try, it is hard to be successful when you're in the wrong place. You go to work unhappy and soon you're coming home unhappy. I have seen people turn a hobby into a successful career just because they loved what they were doing. I have also watched people die a slow death, going to a job they hate every day and thinking they have no choice. I believe we have a purpose, and if you are not living it, you're miserable. When you get on the right path, the world will open up for you."

"It is not as easy as you think, Grammy Ti. You want to do right by your family, so you feel stuck. I couldn't quit my job with the bills that were coming in. I didn't think I had a choice. I wasn't thinking about what my purpose was in life. I was trying to pay the bills. I didn't know you could do both. Isn't it funny that desperation was what finally got me on the right track?"

"That is usually the way," Ti said with a sigh. "We go trudging along, thinking we don't have a choice or any hope, and then, when we are to the point where there is nothing to lose, look for a change. Now you can see that maybe all of this happened for a reason."

"I can see that now. Before, it was easier staying miserable than moving to the unknown. It was comfortable and I knew what I was getting. I worried about rejection and not being capable, so I didn't look for anything else. The irony in all of this is that every day, a part of me felt rejected and inadequate. I didn't even notice until I thought about working there every day, and then I knew it would destroy me piece by piece. I am glad this forced me to look for full-time work, because I could get a job I am excited about. It involves shopping with other people's money." Tricia started laughing.

"See, Patricia, there is a silver lining. Sometimes God answers our prayers, but not in the way we imagine he should. You wanted him to make money magically appear so you could pay your bills. Instead, he put you on a journey to make your whole life better. You are finally looking at living instead of surviving every day. Can you imagine if I had just lent you money? Would that have really fixed everything for you?"

"You know, I never thought of it that way, Grammy. I have changed a lot, going through this, and that would not have happened if you had given me a loan. In fact, we would probably have blown it right away and been back for more. You were right not to lend us the money."

"Hallelujah! Now I feel better. It was so hard to turn you down. I wanted you in my life, and I knew I risked you walking away forever by turning you down. I watched your father get deeper and deeper into trouble with my money. I didn't know how to say no to him. I felt I couldn't go through that with you, even if it meant I would never see you again."

"I am sorry we put you through that. I was so desperate for help. You have given us much more than money could have," Tricia replied.

"You can chime in anytime you want to, Tim," Ti said.

"You know, this has been the hardest month of my life and the best month of my life. I know we have a long way to go, but I am hopeful we will get there. I know it will take years to fix this mess, and we are going to have to make sacrifices. Well, we already have. But both Trish and I want to make it right. So we cut out all the expenses we could, and now we are trying to bump up our income. I earned $60 last night for something I would have done free. I have another job lined up for next week. I will have no problem adding more than $200 a month to our income. And I am having fun doing it."

"That is great, Tim. I am proud of all that you are doing. It feels great to have a part in making life better for your family. I am happy about the increase in your monthly income, because it is going to go toward savings, which we will talk about later. Now, tell me about this job, Patricia."

"Well, Tim and I talked about what I would be happy doing. I am good at shopping, so we looked it up on the Internet. There are so many jobs out there that need my shopping skills. I applied for a couple of them, and there is one that I am in the final three for. I will know on Monday if I got it."

"So, what if it is bad news on Monday?" Grammy Ti asked.

"I thought I would not have any more opportunities if I didn't get this job, but I realize now that it is not the end of the world if I don't. I know there are plenty of positions available, and I will keep trying. The right one for me will come along. I will make the money I need to for my family and I will enjoy going to work. That is a new way of living for me."

"Well, you two earn an A for effort this week. I am proud of you both. It is not easy looking for new work. But it is amazing what happens when you decide to take action. I always believe that when all else fails, do something. Everyone feels better when they take action. Where to begin is the problem. I am so glad you're both on your way. But there is still work to do to get you back on track financially. Let's check on the kids before we tackle the any more finances."

Lessons from Chapter 15

Don't Wait for a Crisis for You to Change

Human beings are creatures of habit. Most of us do not like change. Therefore, we often accept less than we want, as opposed to the unknown. Are you going through life on autopilot? Do you believe that is easier than following your passion? Do you feel imprisoned in your own life?

Instead of thinking about all the reasons you cannot change, think of all the benefits you will enjoy when you do. This applies to everything in your life. You can change anything that you want to. Don't wait for a crisis to force a change; do it for yourself now.

Know That Your Prayers Are Being Answered

Sometimes you need to have faith that what you are going through is for your benefit. Often we can only see that benefit through hindsight. Have faith that everything will work out and that whatever is happening in your life today will make it better for tomorrow. We cannot control what happens in life. We can only control our reaction to what happens.

Anyone who believes in a higher power has gone through a crisis of faith. It often occurs when our prayers appear to go unanswered. It is hard not to get angry. You feel alone and do not trust that a higher power is with you and protecting you.

Know that your prayers are being answered. If you trust in God, know the good that comes to you may be disguised in the form of job loss, disease, or divorce. You may not recognize the benefit immediately. It is hard to trust this process and have faith that it will work out. I could not understand why my financial world was falling apart. I felt that God had abandoned me. I came to realize that by going through the experience, this book was more accurate and I could relate better to those I wanted to help. I had walked a mile in their shoes. There were also many personal benefits for me through this crisis, so I am truly grateful for the experience.

Chapter 16 – Everyone Needs an Emergency Fund

When they finally settled back into the living room, Tim turned to Ti and said, "We are still running $400 behind each month and we have to use our credit cards to cover that. What are we going to do until we get the extra money we need?"

"You are going to have to cut corners even more until you make up that gap. You cannot go further into debt. If that means hot dogs every day, do it. You know it is only for the short term. You are getting so close and you have made so much progress. You don't want to go backward now."

"We just don't have anywhere else to cut expenses, and we don't have much credit left as a safety net. What are we going to do?" Tricia asked, looking defeated. "We are running out of money. I am not sure we will have enough to pay the mortgage at the end of the month."

"You are going to concentrate on the solution instead of the problem. If you concentrate on the problem, you'll feel helpless and won't get anywhere. Know that feeling?" Ti asked.

"I think I have felt helpless for the last year. I was worrying about what would happen if I did anything and what would happen if I didn't. I am not going back. That is a terrible feeling," Tricia said, looking over at Tim for agreement. "But it is hard to concentrate on a solution when you don't know what to do."

"Trish, I have already made $60 and I know next week I will have at least $100 more. We are almost halfway there, so try not to worry. Between the two of us, we will make it happen. We are so close to solving this problem. I think the worst is behind us. Ti, when we get to the point of having extra money, do we pay down the debt or save what is left over?" Tim looked from Tricia to Grammy Ti.

Ti paused before answering. "Well, I have to say there are different answers to that question, depending on which expert you talk to. Some believe you should not save a dime until you have all of your debt paid off. I don't believe in that, so I will give you my opinion and you can decide what is best for the pair of you. My first piece of advice is to have an emergency fund. You may need funds for something that you never thought of, and it can ruin your budget if you don't have them. Without some savings to cover the unexpected, your financial security is always in jeopardy. You never know when something will go wrong with the car, you might be laid off again, or a sinkhole opens in your front yard."

"A sinkhole?" Tim looked confused.

"That was for dramatic effect, Tim. You would never think a sinkhole would open in your yard, but has it happened to anyone? Of course it has. So you prepare for anything life might bring. I like to have $5,000 in my emergency fund, because that is the number that makes me comfortable. There was no equation I followed or calculator I used. It makes me feel like I can handle anything God can throw at me, and I am grateful every day that I have it. I know you are not at a point where you can have $5,000 sitting in a bank account for emergencies. I suggest you start with $500. So, when we get you in a positive cash flow again, the extra money will all go to the emergency fund until you have saved that amount."

"I get the idea of an emergency fund, but I am still not sure if it isn't better to use that to pay off one of the credit cards and just keep that credit card balance available for an emergency. It would save us so much interest." Tricia wanted to make sure they considered every possibility.

"I know it seems like a better idea to pay off your credit card debt, and financially it would probably save you a few bucks in interest. But it won't help you emotionally. You won't have the peace of mind knowing that you have $500 of your own money to help you in case of an emergency. Also, when the credit card debt is gone, it is for good. I don't want you thinking you can use them in an emergency. Besides, it makes it hard to determine what an emergency is with a credit card in your hand. There is nothing like having to hand over cold, hard cash to help you decide if it is an emergency or not. Can you see the difference?"

"Not really, but I am going to trust you. So what happens when we have our $500, and where do we keep it?"

"You want to keep your emergency fund somewhere safe but not too accessible. I keep mine in a separate savings account. The only way I can take money out is to go down to the bank. I can't write a check on it. That way, I have to think twice before making a withdrawal. You need to set up a similar account. It should be one that you can only access by going into the bank and needs both of your signatures for withdrawals. Before you take money from the account, you will have to discuss whether it is an emergency. If it isn't, I trust one or both of you will be smart and say no."

Tim looked at Tricia. "Trish, I think that is a great idea. We could set up the account together and start putting money in as soon as we can. I know I would feel a whole lot better having $500 in the bank. We would have some breathing room. What do you think?"

"Yeah, I agree, Tim. I don't want to have access to it without your knowledge, in case I have a weak moment. I would rather we decide together if we had to use some of the savings. If we both had to go to the bank, I know it would have to be an emergency. It would be a dream to have $500 in the bank at this point. I like the sounds of it more and more. So the first goal is to get a great job and the second goal is to save $500. That sounds easy enough." Tricia gave a lighthearted laugh because she was sure she could do both. It amazed her that she didn't even have any doubts. She was all ready to move on to goal number three. "So what's next?"

"I think that is enough for now. Those are still two big goals, and you're better off taking baby steps than trying to take giant ones. Next week, we will see where you are, and we will talk more about saving versus paying down debt. Your homework is to talk about it at home and come up with pros and cons for both. Then we will figure out the best strategy for you. For now, is anyone hungry?"

Lessons from Chapter 16

Emergency Fund

Do you remember your mother having money stashed away somewhere for emergencies? It could have been in the cookie jar, a coffee tin, or her top drawer. When something unexpected came up, there was money for it. The majority of us do not stash away money for a "rainy day" anymore. We use credit cards instead. Because they are so accessible, it is difficult to determine whether it is a true emergency or not.

The only way to break the credit cycle is to have an emergency fund. It should be accessible but not through a debit card. It should be in an account that has no risk to the principal. Start with $500 and work your way up to six months of your salary. If you must use any funds from this account because of an emergency, your goal is to bring that total back up again as quickly as possible.

Credit Is Not an Option

You have to commit to the rule that credit is not an option. You can't solve your financial problems until you are willing to commit 100 percent. This may be difficult when you get to the end of the money before you get to the end of the week. If you are struggling with your cash budget weekly, divide it into daily amounts. Then you know that in twenty-four hours you have more coming. Remember, during the Depression, credit was not an alternative and they did what was necessary to make it through. You need to do the same.

Chapter 17 - Benefits of Giving

As the afternoon wore on, nobody was in a hurry to go anywhere. They were having fun just talking and telling stories. Ti told Tim and Tricia about her marriage and how she and Tricia's grandfather worked hard providing for their children. Ti wasn't sure if they did their children wrong by concentrating on the providing instead of teaching their children how to manage money.

"I think if I did it again, I wouldn't be handing any money over without a story. I didn't teach my kids anything about saving and tithing, because I just wanted my kids to have everything. I didn't want them to worry about finances like we did. I wanted to protect them, but instead I handicapped them. Please don't do that to Kyle and Sophie. Help them to handle little bits of money, so when they become adults, they can handle the big stuff."

"What is tithing?" Kyle asked.

"Well, Kyle, tithing is giving part of your money back to God," Ti answered.

"God needs money?" Sophie asked curiously. "I thought God could make everything he wanted himself. What would he need money for?"

Ti started to laugh. "I guess I didn't explain that very well. Tithing is giving 10 percent of our money to people who need it, to please God. In my church, people would bring an envelope every Sunday with money and put it in the offering plate. But you don't have to just give to the church. There is nothing that can make me happier than to give money to a person that I know needs it. I give my money to the homeless shelter. They buy food and blankets for people who don't have a home. I also give money to my church every Sunday, and they use it to help all kinds of people. My neighbor Annie likes to give to the Cancer Foundation because her mother and sister had cancer. Her money helps doctors look for a cure so no one else will get sick. You can pick anybody or any group to support. That is the fun of it. Then you go through your life knowing you helped someone. Sharing your wealth gives you a great feeling."

"I was tithing at school last week, Grammy. You would have been proud of me. I tithed half of my sandwich to my best friend Sara because she forgot her lunch. It did feel good to share," Sophie admitted.

"Good for you, Sophie. Now you know why it is good to give. It helps everyone feel better."

"Grammy Ti, we didn't talk about that in our plan. Why?" Tricia wondered.

"It was coming. I wanted you to get your budget balanced before I asked you to help others. I also didn't know how you would feel about tithing. You and your parents did not attend church regularly, so I wasn't sure if you would think I was preaching. It's not that you have to believe in God or follow any religion to give to others, but I learned it in church. I hope you believe in helping others. I do know people who have the attitude that if someone is having a hard time, it is their own fault and they deserve to be there. I don't believe that, and I wasn't sure how you felt."

"We have always tried to help others, Grammy Ti," Tricia said. "I didn't go to church often, but my parents did teach me to always help those in need. I have given in the past, just not regularly. If someone was raising money for a charity at work, I would donate, and I always give money to the Salvation Army at Christmas. So, what is the difference between that and tithing?" It surprised Tricia that her grandmother would think her parents would not teach her to help others.

"Well, Patricia, the difference is that tithing is a set amount each month. Some people give 10 percent, and others give 15 or 20 percent. You could also give a set amount. I like to use percentages, because if I have more, I should give more. Even if it was only a penny, I have given something every month since I was a little girl. It is one of the few things in life that makes me feel good. And on the selfish side, I believe I am building up some good karma. I am only human, you know!"

"I like the idea of giving regularly. I think even if we give only a small amount now, we could increase it along the way. What do you think, Grammy Ti?" Tricia asked.

"Let's get you into a positive cash flow and we will talk about what you want to do. I am glad you think it is a good idea. Your parents did a good job raising you. You've been quiet, Tim. What do you think?"

"Well, I am a little ashamed that I was one of those who believed that if you are in trouble, it was your own fault. Now that I have gone through this, I realize good people make mistakes and need help. I was never one to hand over my hard-earned money to someone else. I think that is wrong. If we didn't have you, we would be in trouble. It could have gotten bad enough that we were homeless, even if only for a week or two. I can see how easy it is to fall on hard times now, and I will never look at homeless people the same again. I think it would be great to help others. I know just passing on your wisdom to the guys at work has made a world of difference."

"You've been telling your co-workers what I have told you?" Ti asked in surprise. "I don't know if that is such a good idea."

"Are you kidding?" Tim responded. "You've been a lifeline for all of us. I found out through conversations at work that many people worry about money. I never thought anyone else in the world would be going through this. It seems that everyone is, to some extent. No one knows what to do about it. It doesn't seem like anyone my age has any money skills. No one ever taught us what to do once we went out and got a job."

"You know, Tim, our generation wasn't taught either. We were just lucky we didn't have the long rope of credit to choke ourselves with. We either had the money or we did without. In fact, I think my generation got so good at doing without that when we had children, we wanted them to have everything. Combine wanting everything with easy access to credit and you have a disaster waiting to happen.

I know everyone is looking for answers, but I am not a professional. I don't want anyone to be worse off because of me."

"Ti, I don't think that is possible. When I look back at what you have taught us, I realize now that much of it is common sense. I sometimes think that is what we are lacking," Tim concluded. "Don't you think, Trish?"

"I don't know if lack of common sense is the problem. I think it was more of not knowing what steps to take once we were in trouble. Once you feel stuck and overwhelmed, you don't know what to do. By talking with us over the last couple of weeks, you have broken down what we need to do in baby steps. I don't think I could have figured that out on my own. I think these steps are simple enough that anyone else can follow them. That is why Tim's friends are listening to your advice as well."

"I still don't know if it is a good idea to share. I am trying to help you out as best I can, but I don't have any formal training. My knowledge comes from experience, and everyone is different. Your friends should be going to a professional, and come to think of it, maybe you should as well."

"There is no way, Ti. You are the best teacher for us. In fact, if you would have passed on your information to Trish's father, and if he had passed it on to us, we may have avoided this altogether. Look at how far we have come. We went from a devastatingly unbalanced budget to being close to balancing it. We have refocused on our careers and are looking at making money doing what we enjoy. We are all happier. We have hope for the future. We may be financially secure one day. None of this was going to happen if there wasn't some intervention. Who else was going to help us? Are there financial crisis counselors out there?"

"Tim, I am sure there are counselors out there. Many people don't seek them out because of embarrassment. Instead, they go to bankruptcy attorneys. Why didn't you two get help earlier?"

"At first I didn't know how bad it was. When I realized we were in trouble and I couldn't fix it myself, I did go to our mortgage broker. He couldn't help us and told me that no one would help us. It was either you or the bankruptcy attorney. It was hard making that phone call to you. It is hard telling anyone that you can't handle your finances and that you are in trouble." Tricia looked first at Tim and then at her grandmother. Talking about it brought back those feelings of humiliation and her face reddened.

"It is hard, Ti. You just feel like such a loser. There is so much emotion tied up with money. Please don't take offense, but I didn't want to come here at all." Tim looked down.

"I guess I can understand that. I can remember not having enough money and feeling like a loser, as you say. I am grateful that you came, even if it was under tough circumstances. It has been great getting to know you again and having company. It is a little bit selfish, but I am glad you only had me to turn to." Ti looked a little embarrassed giving this confession. She was grateful. She had gained a family, and it felt good to help them out. She had enjoyed each week more and more, and the best part was that she felt needed again.

"On that note, we do need to go. It has been a long day, and I am sure the kids are tired. We are grateful for your help, Ti, more than you know. Are you ready, Trish?" Tim stood up.

"Yes. I am tired as well. It has been a long week. Thanks for everything, Grammy Ti." She stood up and walked over to her grandmother and bent down to give her a hug. "I agree with Tim. I don't know what we would do without you. Are you ready, Kyle and Sophie?"

The kids hugged their great-grandmother good-bye and promised to bring her a surprise next week. Tricia and Tim promised to do their homework and have a list of pros and cons on saving versus repaying the debt. They also promised to come back with a balanced budget. As they walked out the door, Tricia looked back and saw her grandmother waving. She now saw the sadness on her grandmother's face that her children had seen the week before. Perhaps they were helping her grandmother as much as she was helping them.

Lesson from Chapter 17

Tithing

Tithing is a ritual recorded throughout history and believed to encourage those in society who have more, to give to those who are less fortunate. It was a symbol to God of gratitude for all the abundance he placed in one's life. Most organized religions incorporate some form of tithing.

We associate tithing with the church, but it can be any consistent form of charity. When we give to others, we are helping ourselves as well. We feel better for doing it. We have more appreciation for our life. We know we are making a difference for our fellow man.

In the material on the law of attraction, there are many examples of the universe responding to giving. Often you get back more than you give. I believe that tithing is good for society, for you, and for the beneficiary. You can see the benefits by making a commitment to tithing your money regularly.

Chapter 18 – If at First You Don't Succeed, Try Again

Sunday was family day. Tricia could not believe how much time they spent together as a family now. Before, it was always about going out and doing errands or being at home in separate rooms. They were together but they didn't interact. She realized now how much fun she was having hanging out with the kids and Tim.

After putting the kids to bed, Tricia found Tim in the den, writing on a pad of paper. "What are you doing?" she asked.

"Well, I decided I was going to make a flyer advertising my services and prices so I could pass them out at work. I was trying to decide what services would be practical to do at home. I don't have a garage like a mechanic; nor do I have all the tools that I need. I want to make sure I can do the job with what I have."

"The flyer is a great idea, Tim. It will also make it easier for you if you decide the price ahead of time. Then you won't feel like you need to change it based on whether it is a close friend or not."

"That is what I was thinking. It is hard dealing with friends. I thought I would set a fair price that was less than going to a professional mechanic. I was also thinking I might go talk to Mike at the garage and see if I can work out a referral system. Maybe he will give people a break on the price if I send them to him for the repairs I can't do. I think it would be great if I have people coming to me with all of their car needs, and then I can decide if I can do it or Mike can."

"You know, it almost sounds like a full-time job to me. You better make sure you don't take on too much. You only need to make an extra $200 each month, you know. I want to make sure we keep having our family time together. I like how we spent time with the kids today. I don't want to lose that. If I get that full-time job, it will mean more work here at home for you as well."

"Don't worry, Trish, I already thought about all of that. I thought that I would only work Tuesdays, Wednesdays, and Saturdays. We still have Friday date night and Sunday to hang out as a family. I can be in charge of dinner on Mondays and Thursdays, so it should all work out. I want to get out of this financial mess as quickly as possible, and I love working on cars. You know that."

"Yeah, I know, and that is why I feel I had to say something. I don't want to go back to when cars were more important than family. I want to balance family and our jobs."

"Don't worry, Trish. It is going to work out, I promise. I want that too. If I am getting too wrapped up in repairing these cars, let me know. I will do the same for you. Okay?"

"That's a deal. Now I have to think about the big phone call tomorrow. I really want this job." Tricia sat down on the couch beside Tim. "I can't believe how excited I am. I think this job would be perfect. I can learn in the department, and if I work hard, I can move up in the company. I never looked at having a career before. I can't believe how much I have changed."

"It has all been for the better. I see a whole new you. You have been beaming lately and you are smiling and laughing. That was how you were when I met you. Then life just seemed to take that away from you. It is so great to see you happy."

"It feels great to be happy, Tim. I can't believe I am saying this, but I am glad we got into this trouble. Even though we are still broke and I still worry that we will never get out of this mess, I feel like I have a second chance. Not many people get to experience that. Money problems usually tear people apart, not build them up. How did we get so lucky?"

"I think your grandmother has a lot to do with it. I think it is easier to face this with someone guiding you along. She also doesn't take any crap, which—although it has been embarrassing at times—has been good for me. She has kept us from feeling sorry for ourselves and made us face everything head on. We didn't even get the luxury of blaming someone else. That has stopped many fights right there. Every time I fall into the trap of getting mad, I just hear your grandmother's voice saying 'grow up, Tim.' It is hard to tune her out." Tim started to laugh.

"I hear that same voice. I hear 'you are better than that, Patricia.' She is a godsend. Here I thought she was so mean, and yet she is a great person. I have enjoyed hanging out at her place. I was thinking that we should invite her here one day a week. She seems lonely, and we can gain even more wisdom by seeing her more often." Tricia also knew the kids would be all for it.

"It's funny you mention that. Did you see the look on her face when we left? I felt so guilty," Tim agreed.

"Yeah, I saw it too. She seemed so sad when we were leaving. What if we have her here every Wednesday, and we will make sure that we have a nice dinner that night. It could be good for us as well, because we will stay focused and make more progress on our finances."

"I think that is a great idea. You should call her tomorrow. Right now, I need to get this flyer finished. I want to have it ready so I can ask Helen in the office tomorrow if she will photocopy it for me. Then I can hand it out to everyone. I'll need a calendar or appointment book, though. Do we have one around here?"

"I think there is one in the hall table drawer. I bought it to keep track of our schedules and the kids' activities, but I never used it. We need to keep track of what each of us is doing. Should we put a calendar on the fridge?" Tricia wondered.

"Let's wait until tomorrow to see if you get the job. Once we get a handle on your hours, I will work around them. Did they mention anything about the hours you would be working?" Tim looked over at Tricia. He couldn't believe how much she had changed. Her features had softened and her eyes had the sparkle that he had fallen in love with. He didn't think either had been aware of how hard the past year had been on them.

"I will be working daytime hours. There may be days that I will have to work later, but most days I should be home by five. I am sure we will be able to work it out. I am tired and ready for bed, so I am going to go up and leave you to your flyer." Tricia walked over and kissed Tim good night.

Monday morning was a flurry of lunch bags and backpacks. It seemed everyone was running behind schedule; Tricia drove Tim to work and the kids to school. When she got home, all she wanted was some peace and quiet. She knew that it would be a long day, waiting for the phone call, so she had intentionally overscheduled her day. There had been little time last week to get the housework done, so she was trying to catch up. She didn't know how she was going to do it working full time.

By lunchtime, she had made a dent in her to-do list. She thought about setting up a schedule for housework. That way, regardless of which one got home first, they would know what to do. It would be easier if they had a meal schedule as well.

Tricia sat down with a scrap piece of cardboard left behind from one of the kids' school projects and drew a mock calendar. She thought about the list she had today and what order would be best to follow throughout the week. She was printing each chore on a small square of paper when the phone rang.

Tricia was nervous, answering the phone. She wanted this job very much. Unfortunately, the answer wasn't what she had hoped for. The head of human resources told her she had done a great job, but one of the other candidates had more experience. They would keep her information on file and let her know if another position became available. Tricia hung up the phone and sat down. She didn't know how to feel. On the one hand, they liked her and she was only beaten out on experience. On the other hand, how was she to get a job in a field where she had no experience?

She decided that she would finish her calendar and then go back online to look for something else. She wasn't going to give up. Now that she knew the job she wanted, nothing else would do. She spent the afternoon searching for positions and attaching her résumé to the applications. She also sent a thank-you note to the company that turned her down. She felt thankful for the interview opportunity and the confidence that she gained from the experience.

She had not noticed that the afternoon had passed, and Tim and the kids coming through the door startled her. Tim must have waited at the bus stop for them on his way home. He came bounding up the stairs looking for her.

"Well, what happened?" Tim was full of excitement.

"I didn't get it," Tricia replied. "It's okay; I'm okay. I have spent the afternoon applying for other positions. They liked me, but the other candidate had more experience. I at least now know what I want to be when I grow up."

"Oh, honey, I am so sorry. I thought you would get that job. I was all ready to celebrate. I have been thinking about you all day. But look at you. You are okay. I am so proud of you. So we can't celebrate a new job, so let's celebrate you being all grown up." Tim grabbed her and gave her a hug. "I bought root beer."

The kids jumped up and down and starting chanting, "Root beer floats!" They moved the party into the kitchen, and all worked together making the floats look as festive as possible. Tim told Tricia that he had scheduled another job working on brakes for a co-worker's brother. He was excited that other people outside work wanted his help as well. He had booked the job for Saturday, and they agreed on $100 for the work. He also had Wednesday after work booked for an oil change that would earn him $20. He was so happy that Tricia couldn't help but feel better. Even though she had did not get the job she had wanted, she and her family were fine.

"I am so proud of you. You had two choices when you found out about the mess we were in. You could have left me and all of this mess behind. For some people, I am sure they would see that as the best alternative. But you chose to stay and work this out. I see how committed you are to this, and it makes me want to try even harder."

Tim reached out for her hand. "Trish, it crossed my mind for about one second to leave this mess behind. But I know in my heart I would be happier broke with you than wealthy on my own, so it wasn't a hard choice at all. I wish you would have a little more faith in our marriage. I am proud of you. You are the one who has kept us going. I am sure we would have lost everything if I had been taking care of the finances."

"I don't think so, but thanks for the vote of confidence. I was thinking about going to the mall after work tomorrow and seeing if there isn't some part-time work available at one of the stores. At least I could get my foot in the door and it would increase our household income. What do you think?"

"I think that is a great idea. You never know who you will meet and what opportunity will come up. Remember what Ti said, 'Do something, anything.'"

"Speaking of her, I think I should call her and let her know what happened with the job. I am sure she is wondering, and it is a long way to Saturday when we see her again. Would you mind starting supper while I give her a call?"

"I don't mind at all. Remember, we were talking about inviting her to dinner on Wednesday. Why don't you ask if she is free?"

"I had forgotten about that. You know, I think I will. I will be right back to help you. Do you kids have homework?" She turned to the kids, who had foam from the floats on their lips, pretending they were mustaches. They were laughing and carrying on, and Tricia hated to break up the party.

"I don't have any," said Kyle.

"Me neither," said Sophie.

"Finish your root beer floats in here with Dad, and I will be back in a minute. Then you can help me set the table."

The kids went back to working on their mustaches, and Tim turned to the fridge to begin supper. Tricia went into the den to call Grammy Ti. When she sat down, she remembered how she felt making that first phone call. She had never been so nervous or humiliated. She had been desperate and made a phone call that changed her life. Looking back, she had wondered why she had been so afraid. In fact, she had noticed that she was doing many things now that had terrified her before.

Ti picked up on the first ring because she was standing beside the phone in the kitchen. She had been at that spot for the past ten minutes, trying to decide what she was going to make herself for dinner. It was difficult to cook for one, and everything looked unappetizing to her. When she recognized Tricia's voice on the other end, she was a little shocked. "Patricia, is everything all right?" she asked.

"Grammy, everything is fine. I just wanted to let you know that I didn't get the position today. I am disappointed, but I figure something else will come up. I have only been at this for a week."

"I am so sorry to hear that, dear. I know you wanted that job. What are you going to do now?"

Tricia thought for a moment. She didn't know whether she should burden her grandmother, but she wanted her opinion. She decided that her advice so far had been valuable and it would be great to hear what she had to say. "Well, I was thinking about going to the mall to hand out my résumé, to see if there might be some opportunities in one of the stores there. What do you think?"

"I think that is a great idea. It is another step toward getting the job you want. I am proud of you," Ti said softly. She had become fond of Tricia and her family, and she wanted her to succeed.

"Thanks, Grammy. That does mean a lot to me. Before I go, we wanted to invite you to dinner on Wednesday night. I could pick you up after work. We thought you would like to see the home that nearly did us in," Tricia kidded.

"Are you sure, Patricia? It is out of your way," Ti responded.

"It is not that much out of the way, and we would love to have you. We thought you might like the company, and none of us want to wait until Saturday to see you."

"Well, that would be great. I will see you then."

"See you on Wednesday. Good-bye."

"Good-bye and give the kids a hug for me."

Tricia hung up after promising to pass the hugs along. She felt better after talking to her grandmother, especially when she said she was proud of her. Tricia had not expected that.

Halfway across town, Ti hung up the phone gently. She couldn't believe that they had invited her over on Wednesday. She had been so lonely, and Saturdays were such a joy. To see them Wednesday as well seemed like a gift. She was suddenly starving and decided to make a great big meal for herself in celebration.

"She is coming on Wednesday," Tricia remarked as she walked into the kitchen. "I am going to pick her up after work."

"Who is coming on Wednesday?" Kyle asked.

"Grammy Ti is coming for dinner. What do you think about that?"

"That would be great, Mom. We have so much fun with her. Can we teach her how to play cards?"

"I am sure she knows all the card games in the world, and she may even be able to teach you a new one," Tricia replied with a smile.

"That would be so cool," Kyle said.

Tricia walked over to the stove, where Tim was making pasta sauce. They were eating pasta a lot lately, but the kids liked it. It worked out well, because it was cheap and easy. "Need any help?" Tricia asked him.

"No, I'm good. It will be ready in about ten minutes, so you can set the table if you like. First the kids need to clean up their root beer mess. I think they enjoyed that a little too much. What else did your grandmother say?"

"She said she was proud of me. That was a shock. It has been amazing how close we have gotten so quickly. It is sad that I have wasted so much time not knowing her. Having her in our lives is great for the kids as well. With your parents away and my mother missing in action, they haven't had the extended family experience."

"I agree," Tim said as he drained the pasta. "Everyone needs a grandmother. Are we ready to eat?"

Lessons from Chapter 18

Do Something, Anything

I remember growing up and hearing "God helps those who help themselves." I believe that. If you get up and start working on your problems, in whatever way you can, you will put into motion the changes that will help you reach your goal.

Feeling stuck or paralyzed is the biggest barrier to getting out of financial difficulty. You need to do something. Action is the only solution to change. Make a list of anything you can think of that could help you change your situation. Every day, do one item on your list. Reward yourself if you need to. If you do that, the action you take will set off a chain reaction that will move you closer and closer to solving your problems. Do something, anything.

If at First You Don't Succeed, Try Again

No one is lucky enough to have life go their way all the time. You need to keep trying. There are many stories about successful people who wouldn't give up and suffered many rejections before getting what they wanted. Don't look at a "no" as a step back. Look at it as getting closer to finding what will work. There is always a way. Just keep on trying. Many times, in hindsight, we discover the "no" was the best thing that could happen to us.

Chapter 19 – Savings versus Debt Reduction

At dinner, the family discussed the menu for Wednesday's dinner with Grammy Ti. The kids wanted to decorate the house, but Tricia convinced them it may scare off their grandmother if they make too much of a big deal about it. It was best to make the house neat and tidy but not overdo it.

After the kids were in bed, Tricia and Tim sat down to do their homework. They were hoping that if they had everything ready for Wednesday night, they could share it with Ti then. This should speed up their progress. They needed to list the pros and cons of saving versus paying down the debt. Neither was sure where to start.

"What do you think about it, Trish? I don't know anything about this stuff. I think we should concentrate on paying down the debt. That is the biggest worry right now. Why bother putting money away?"

"I think we should get a piece of paper and put 'Save' on one side and 'Debt' on the other. Underneath them, we will list pros and cons. Let's look at saving first. One of the pros of saving is feeling more secure having money in the bank. What do you think?"

"I agree with that. Another pro would be that we could eventually save for something specific so we can pay cash for it. We could save for a Corvette, for instance." Tim winked at Tricia.

Tricia pretended she didn't hear the Corvette comment. "Another pro would be that we could feel like we are moving forward. I think that only concentrating on the debt will keep us too much in the past. Can you think of any other pros?"

They both sat there silently, then Tim spoke up. "I think it would be good to get some money tucked away for the kids' college expenses, and we do want to retire one day."

"But how can we save money for something so far away when we are up to our eyeballs in debt?" Tricia asked.

"Well, that would be one of the cons. It takes away from paying down the debt faster. But look how fast the last ten years went by. Kyle will be in college in another ten years. That isn't long. We can save a little bit each year or a whole lot later."

"Okay," Tricia agreed. "We have saving for specifics, moving forward, and long-term goals in the pros, and taking away from the debt repayment in the cons. Can you think of any other pros?"

"I think the biggest pro is being able to sleep better at night. I know that if I had money in the bank, as well as paying our debts, I would sleep better. We don't have any control over what the credit card companies do. They could raise our interest rate tomorrow to 30 percent, and there is nothing we can do about it. So that scares me. But I feel having money in the bank gives me power. I have some control. That is what I want. I want to feel like I have choices."

"I agree, Tim. It would make me feel better as well. But I have to say I am torn because I feel stressed about having all this debt. I want to pay it down as quickly as possible, and it will take longer if we start a savings program."

"Let's not forget that you don't earn much in a savings account," Tim added.

"I don't even know what interest rates a bank pays. Do you, Tim? We need to look into that as well. Let's move on to debt. What are the pros of paying off the debt? I guess the first on the list is peace of mind." Tricia wrote under the debt column.

"I think we should ask your grandmother about savings accounts. I don't know anything about that. I would say under debts you should put *saving interest*. That is important. I can't think of any cons, can you?"

"Not really. I am leaning toward putting most of the money to debt, but I want to get that emergency fund started. I am going to put this list on the fridge, and if we think of anything, we can put it in the proper column. Sound good?" Tricia looked up at Tim. He was staring at her and had the weirdest look on his face. "What?" she asked.

Tim turned a little pink. "I was just enjoying watching you do your homework. You look so cute when you are thinking. You wrinkle up your nose and chew on the end of the pencil. I am sure all the boys in grade school loved you." He smiled.

"Yeah, sure they did. With my pigtails and braces, I was a real beauty," Tricia kidded, but she felt a little embarrassed that he was staring at her. "Aren't you glad you met me after that awkward stage?"

Tim leaned over and kissed her. "I sure am," he said with a smile. "But I still bet the guys went wild over you, braces and all."

Wednesday came more quickly than anyone could imagine, and when Tricia looked at the list on the fridge, she noticed that nothing had been added. She hoped they could complete it with her grandmother's help tonight. She was looking forward to seeing her grandmother again. As she was walking out the door, the phone rang. She was going to let it ring but decided it could be Ti. She ran back inside and grabbed the phone.

"Hello," she panted.

"May I speak to Patricia Smith please?"

"Speaking," Tricia said not hiding the disappointment in her voice. She was going to be late for work because of a telemarketer.

"Patricia, this is Kate Helms from Burkhart and Associates. You have applied for the position in purchasing?"

"Yes. Yes I have, Kate."

"Well, Melanie Lancaster, the head of purchasing, would like to set up an interview with you. Will you be available tomorrow?"

"I will. What time would she like to meet?" Tricia was trying hard to remain calm.

"How does 9:00 AM work for you?"

"That would be fine. Where is her office?"

Savings versus Debt Reduction

"She is at the downtown location at Fifth and Main. Do you know where that is?"

"Yes I do. I will be there at nine sharp. Thank you so much. Is there anything I should bring with me?"

"No. She will have a copy of your résumé, and I believe that is all she needs. I will let her know you will be there tomorrow morning. Thank you. Good-bye."

"Good-bye." Tricia almost sang it. She had another interview. She looked at the list of pros and cons on the fridge, and she had written the information for her interview all over it. No matter. If she got this job, she would have enough money for debt and savings. She almost skipped out the door.

Grammy Ti was the first person she told about the interview. They had talked about it in the car and continued talking about it as they walked into the kitchen.

"What's all the excitement about?" Tim asked.

"I have another interview," Tricia replied as she ran over to him and hugged him. She left her grandmother standing awkwardly at the doorway. Kyle and Sophie ran into the room to see what the fuss was and ran over to their great-grandmother.

"Grammy Ti," they screamed together, and they both threw their arms around her. She laughed and hugged them both back. She didn't even know these two a couple of months ago, and now she was getting this reaction from them. Sometimes things just worked out.

"Now, don't go knocking poor Grammy Ti over. At least let her get in the kitchen." Tim kissed Tricia and then walked toward Ti. "Here, you can sit right here before they knock you over," Tim said with a laugh. He held out a kitchen chair for her.

"Thanks, Tim. What an exciting household tonight. I am so happy to be a part of it."

The conversation flew around the kitchen, from kids to parents to grandmother. Everyone got caught up on what had happened during the day, and there was a festive atmosphere. Tim quickly got dinner on the table, but food did nothing to slow the conversation down.

"You must be ready to go home by now, Ti. I am exhausted and I am used to this craziness." Tim looked over his shoulder at Ti.

Lessons from the Depression

He invited her to sit at the table with Tricia while he and the kids cleaned up.

"No, Tim. I miss this. Suppertime was always my favorite. I loved hearing everyone's stories from the day. It is times like these that make you feel like part of a family."

"I guess so," Tim replied. "But sometimes I would love to have a quiet dinner."

"You will, Tim, and then you will miss this," Ti stated. She hated eating dinner alone in her quiet home. Tim didn't know what a blessing all this chaos was.

Tim got the kids off doing homework and reading, and then sat down with Tricia and Ti to discuss their own homework. "Well, you messed this up, Trish," Tim commented, looking at their list. "Can you even read what our pros and cons are?"

"I would like to talk about it, if you don't mind, Grammy. We did write down points, but neither of us felt confident doing that. Can you tell us what you think?"

"I will tell you what little I know, and then you will have to decide. First off, there is no one right way to do this. There are two parts to money, emotional and financial. Sometimes it may be financially better to do it one way, but it would be hard to do emotionally. What's the use of having more pennies in the bank if you are spending your nights awake worrying? So you need to balance both of these. You want to feel confident and comfortable with your decisions."

"I think that is why we were having a problem with this. Our heads and our stomachs are telling us to do something different," Tricia explained.

"It is sometimes difficult working it out between those two, but you can if you come up with a compromise that tries to satisfy a part of both. So, when you have a high-interest credit card, it is important to pay it off as quickly as possible, because the interest is compounding against you. But as I said before, it gives you great peace of mind to have money in the bank. How can you do both when you have a limited amount of money? You decide which is more important to you and put more money toward that. When you think about having your credit card paid off versus having money in the bank, which one makes you feel better?" Ti looked at Tricia first and then over at Tim.

Tricia thought about it for a moment. "I want to decrease our debt. That would be my priority. But I do like the thought of having money in the bank. I think if we can put away $500, add a little to that every week, and use the rest to pay down the debt, I would be happy. What about you, Tim?"

"I was thinking about this last night. Once you get your job and we know your income, I would like to set up a plan where we save $500 for our emergency fund and then split up the extra money. I was thinking 50 percent going to debt, 25 percent going to short-term savings, and 25 percent going to longer-term savings like the kids' education and our retirement. It just gives me the feeling that our money is working harder for us in the long term, even though we will pay more interest in the short term. If we make extra money above that, we could commit to using that to pay the debt. I know I will make more than $200 a month fixing cars on the side, so the extra could go on the credit cards. What do you think about that, Ti?"

"As I said before, Tim, there isn't just one right way. But this sounds well thought out to me. You may want to think about changing the percentages a little, because your interest costs are so high. What if you were to put 15 percent into both saving categories and put 70 percent toward your debt?"

"I like that idea, Tim. I want to get rid of the debt. We could raise the percentages that are going to savings next year after we have made a dent in the credit cards." Tricia felt strongly about cutting out the debt.

"I guess that would be all right. I just feel better when I have money in the bank. I guess that is the emotional side," Tim agreed.

"The best way to decide is to use a calculator and see how the numbers come out. Why don't I go visit with the kids and you two go up to the computer and try different ways to use that monthly amount. You can go onto any bank Web site and it will have a calculator you can use to show you how long it will take to pay off your debts with different payment amounts. There are also calculators to show how much your savings can grow."

"How do you know about all of this?" Tim asked.

"I have too much time on my hands," Ti answered with a smile.

"Let's go, Tim. We will meet you back here in fifteen minutes, Grammy Ti."

Tricia and Tim headed upstairs, knowing that Ti and the kids would find something fun to do in their absence. Now that they had thought about the pros and cons of saving money versus paying down debt, they were eager to know how the numbers would look. They were sure it was going to be a tight contest between the financial numbers and their emotional needs.

Lessons from Chapter 19

Emotional versus Financial

A common mistake in making personal financial decisions is not recognizing that there are two sides to money. Most people only consider what the numbers or the financial aspects are. They base their decisions strictly on what the financial outcome is, instead of considering how those strategies make them feel.

The best financial strategy will not work if you do not carry it out. This does not mean you avoid a strategy because it is difficult. But you should not carry through with an investment decision that causes you to lose sleep or increases your anxiety. Find a balance between what works financially and what you feel comfortable with, and you will be successful.

Forget about the Joneses

It is time to decide what is best for your family. It does not matter what anyone else thinks. Do what is necessary to get your finances in order. Bring financial security back to your family. Results produce confidence. When you become confident with what you are doing, you will have people ask for your advice. Forget about the Joneses—your family rocks!

Chapter 20 – Making an Automatic Plan

It was almost half an hour later before Tim and Tricia were back in the kitchen. They found Ti having milk and cookies with the kids and talking about some character on TV.

"Well, I can see you missed us," Tricia laughed. "What are you guys talking about? We could hear you all the way upstairs."

"We are just debating whether *Kids around the World* is more fun to watch than *Dangerous Dinosaurs*. So, what did you find out?" Ti was enjoying the bewildered look on Tim and Tricia's faces. They had no idea she would know about these TV shows.

"Well, we learned quickly how much we need to put toward the debt to make it go away. It was cool trying different scenarios. Sorry it took so long, although it is great that you are sharing your vast knowledge with the kids as well," Tim replied with a big smile.

"It was well worth the wait, getting to spend time with these two. I can't wait to see what you have come up with."

"You know, it was fun doing the calculations, Ti. We got to see what our life would be like with whatever decision we made. I wish we could do that with everything in life," Tim said.

"If you thought about that for a moment, you probably wouldn't want that. Can you imagine having to go through that with every decision? You would never live your life and you would never enjoy the element of surprise," Ti responded.

Making an Automatic Plan

"Well, it still would be fun with some things, I think." Tim winked at Ti and then looked at Tricia.

"Let's get back on track," Tricia interrupted. "We looked at the credit card debt separately from the mortgage. The average interest rate on the credit cards is 15 percent. The minimum payment total is almost $1,400 a month, and that has them paid off in about four years. We will have another $200 to pay debt or save with, if we never go to the mall again."

"Do we have to go over that again, Trish?" Tim thought that issue was dead and gone.

"I am just kidding, Tim." Tricia winked at him. "If we put the whole amount on the debt, we will have all the cards paid off in about three years and then we could start saving the full $1,600. Ten years from now, we will have over $190,000 saved at a return of 10 percent a year. If we put the minimum toward the debt and the $200 in savings, it would take longer to reduce our debt, but we would have money saved right away. In ten years, we will pay more interest, but our savings will increase about $4,000."

"I know it is confusing when you are looking at these numbers. When you take everything into account, there isn't much difference. I think you are missing the most important fact. You are going from having no plan, except for bankruptcy, to paying off your credit card debt and having all that money saved in only ten years. Do you realize what a great story that is? I think you need to just take a moment and think about that, because ten years goes by so quickly. With either plan, you are going to have a great future. Remember when the future was bleak, Patricia?" Ti looked over at her granddaughter. She was so proud of the two of them, and she didn't know what to do with all this emotion she felt. This was as close to a miracle as she had ever witnessed.

"You know, you are right, Grammy Ti. I can't believe that we have come so far that we now just take for granted that everything is going to work out. When did that happen? I know *why* it happened. It is all because of you. We would never been able to get this far without you. You are right. Both of these take us to a great ending. If you feel better about the money in the bank, Tim, we will start saving the $200. I am just going to work hard to find an extra $200

Lessons from the Depression

in the budget to put on the debt so I can have both. You know I always want it all," Trisha said with a giggle. "I think that calls for more milk and cookies before we take Grammy Ti home. What do you think, kids?" Both Sophie and Kyle nodded eagerly.

"So, what is our homework for next week?" Tim asked as he refilled the glasses with milk and set out more cookies.

"Well, a plan isn't any good unless you put it into action. You need to get automatic payment plans going for the credit cards and set up an investment plan. Do you know how you are going to invest the money? At 10 percent, you are going to have to take a risk," Grammy Ti pointed out.

"We thought we would open a separate savings account for the $500 first. We are going to set it up so we both have to sign for withdrawals and we can't access the funds through the bank machine. Once the $500 is in the bank, we are going to look for somewhere to invest longer term. Do you know anything about investing?" Tricia looked up at her grandmother, hoping she would help them with the last piece of the puzzle.

"I am not an expert, but I have an expert that I deal with whom I trust. She has been a financial adviser for over twenty years, and she is good at making sure the investment matches the goal. If you want, I can have her call you and set up an appointment. You can also ask your friends and co-workers, to see who they would recommend. I would interview two or three advisers to see that you are compatible. You want to make sure that you feel comfortable asking questions and stating your own opinions. Too many people let others run their affairs and then wonder why it does not work out. No one loves your money more than you do, so you have to stick up for it. You don't want someone who talks over your head or is high pressure. Also, make sure it is someone with experience and that they have excellent credentials. I had a kid call me on the phone the other day, wanting me to invest with him. I know everyone has to start somewhere, but he had no training except for the company's three-month introduction program. He didn't have any degrees, diplomas, or designations. I just didn't feel comfortable dealing with him. Well, that and the fact that he was a stranger on the phone," Ti chuckled. "He thought he had a stupid old woman on the hook, but I straightened him out."

Both Tricia and Tim joined in the laughter. No one would take advantage of Ti. That was obvious. They also knew that if an adviser passed the "Ti test," they would be worth meeting. Both took her advice seriously. They wanted to deal with someone they could trust and feel comfortable with.

"I would like to meet your adviser. What about you, Trish?" Tim asked.

"Yes I would, and the sooner the better. Ask around at work as well, Tim. I like the idea of interviewing a couple of people. I want to make sure we can find someone we feel comfortable working with. Well, have we tired you out yet, Grammy Ti? I think we had better get you home. Could you arrange for your adviser to meet us at your house on Saturday? Does she work on Saturdays?"

"I don't think she usually does, but I am sure if she is available, she will stop by. It is short notice, though. If not, I will try to set it up for next week. Don't forget about your homework. Set up all of your payments automatically so you are never late. Get the savings account set up and then work on making more money. Now, I think I have finished my work here. My bed is calling me so, if you don't mind, I will call it a night."

"Awwwww," Kyle and Sophie chimed in together. "We don't want you to go."

"I know, kids, but I am an old lady and I need my beauty sleep and so do you. Don't you have school tomorrow? You can't learn with a tired brain, and your mother has her interview tomorrow. Also, you're coming to my house Saturday, and I have something special planned for you."

"Can we stay again, like last time?" Sophie asked.

"Sophie, you know that isn't polite. And besides, you will wear Grammy out," Tricia scolded.

"You know, Patricia, I would love to have them overnight again. I can't Friday night, but I could take them Saturday night."

"Yeah!" shouted Sophie. "Can we, please?"

"What do you think, Tim?"

"I don't mind. They outnumber us anyways. We may as well go with the flow."

Getting Ti out to the car was a long, drawn-out affair. The kids didn't want to let go of her, and Trish had to promise them a special bedtime story to get them to head upstairs. When Tim got back, the kids were asleep and Trish was getting ready for bed herself.

"Well, Trish? Are we on our way yet?"

"Tim, I am so excited. I can't believe how much our lives have changed in just a few short months. I know the next twenty years are not going to be easy, but I am ready to save all of that money."

"I don't think it is going to be that hard. We have finally taken a good look at our lives and decided what is important to us. We were going out and buying stuff that was a waste of money because we thought we should or we had to or it would make us feel better. Those times are over. Now we have control. We are making choices based on what is right for us. Is there a better life than that?"

"I think it's a good one. I am wiped out after tonight, but it was fun. I am off to bed so I can be ready to tackle this interview tomorrow. Coming?" Tricia said to Tim.

"Yep, too much fun makes Tim a tired boy."

They both laughed and headed off to bed.

Lessons from Chapter 20

Setting Up a Plan

Any plan is a good plan as long as you put it into action. There are various financial Web sites that can help you calculate different scenarios so you can decide what the best course of action is for you. The power of compounding can work for you or against you, and it is in your best interest to know how it will affect the outcome.

After you have determined the amount available to save or put toward the debt, use the calculators to see how it affects the long-term numbers. Once you find the best financial strategy, talk to your partner about how that strategy feels emotionally. Try to balance these two.

Automatic Payments for Bills and Cash for Discretionary Spending

To keep you on track and to ensure your payments are on time, start automatic payments through your financial institution. Make sure that you have the money in the account to cover these payments, because the insufficient funds fees are high. Budget your weekly amount to go to your payments knowing the cash left over is what you will use for household expenses.

Debit cards can spoil a budget. You should use cash instead. Leave the correct amount in your account to cover all automatic payments and withdraw the rest to cover your discretionary spending. This would include items like food, entertainment, car costs, and spending money. Separate the cash into envelopes so you use the correct amount for each category. You will find that using cash will save you money, because you are more apt to think twice before spending it. You know that once it is gone, you have nothing until the following week. Cash also prevents you from spending more than you make.

Once you have agreed on a plan, set it into action. Set up your payments automatically. Make sure you transfer the money each month into your savings account. Review this every couple of months to ensure that it still works. Circumstances can change, so you need to be able to adapt the plan to those changes. Once the plan is set up, it should be easy to maintain.

Chapter 21 – Having a Positive Attitude

Tricia got up early so she had plenty of time to get ready for her interview. She wore the same gray suit she had worn to her last interview, but put on a pink blouse for good luck. She was ready to go long before anyone else was awake, so she went over some notes she had made on the company. By the time Tim got up, she was feeling very confident.

"Well, well, well, look at you. You look great, Trish. How do you feel?" Tim thought she looked perfect for the interview.

"I feel great, Tim. I am not nervous at all. I know I am going to get a job that I like. If it is not with this company, then I will have another interview that will get me the job with the right company." Trisha smiled up at Tim.

"Go get 'em, tiger!" Tim squeezed Tricia's shoulder. "I know you will do grrrrrrrreat!"

They both started laughing at Tim's horrible Tony the Tiger impression. The kids came running into the kitchen, wondering what was going on.

"What are you guys laughing about, Mom?" Kyle asked.

"Dad was just being silly, hon," Tricia replied.

"Mommy, you look so pretty," Sophie said, wide-eyed.

"Thanks, Sophie. Do you think that this is right for my interview?"

"Oh yes, Mommy. You look awesome."

The kitchen became a hubbub of activity as Tricia and Tim got the kids and themselves ready for the day ahead. As they headed out the door, Tim gave Tricia's hand a squeeze and wished her good luck.

At the interview, Tricia felt calm and confident. The questions asked were similar to the ones in the previous interview. It was different this time, because she did not feel as if this was her only shot. She knew that she had a lot to offer this company, and if they didn't see that, then another company would. The interview ended on a positive note, and they promised to get back to her in a day or so.

On her drive home, Tricia took the scenic route. She was in no hurry to go anywhere. She was feeling good about the interview and even better about her life. Nothing had changed but her attitude. She was still poor and had more money going out the door than coming in, but she now had hope. She now had a plan. She now had a grandmother. Life was good.

After finishing her errands and doing some grocery shopping, Tricia finally made it home. It was already after two, and she had so much to do before the kids came home. She quickly put the food away and started a load of laundry. It wasn't until she came back into the kitchen that she noticed the flashing light on the phone. She dialed in for the messages and the first one shocked her.

"Patricia, this is Melanie Lancaster. Please call me back as soon as you get this message."

Tricia almost dropped the phone. Was this good or bad? Melanie had sounded a little annoyed on the phone, but she had a tendency to sound like that. Tricia's hand shook as she dialed the number.

"Hi Melanie, this is Patricia. I am returning your call."

"Patricia, I am so glad you got the message. I was worried because I had left it on your machine several hours ago. You were my last interview for this position, and I knew almost instantly that you were the one I wanted to work with. I know you are a little short on experience, but your confidence and your positive attitude won me over. Anyone can learn the job. You can't teach attitude. Are you still interested in the position?"

"Absolutely," Tricia almost shouted into the phone.

"There's that positive spirit again," Melanie said. "Can we get together on Monday and discuss the details?"

"I am working on Monday until three. Can we meet after that?"

"Sure, let's make it for four. How many weeks' notice will you need to give?"

"I will talk to my boss at work on Monday, and I will let you know at our meeting. He is a good guy, so I am sure that he will help me out. When would you like me to start?"

"I was hoping we could get some training going next week. What if we trained you part time for two weeks, working around your present schedule, and then you can start full time after that? Would that be enough notice?"

"I am sure I can work it out. I don't want to leave him high and dry. It has been slow lately, so I am not even sure he will hire a replacement. That will make the transition a whole lot easier for the company. He has been good to me, so I would like to make sure I give him proper notice."

"No problem. See you Monday at four."

"Thank you so much, Melanie. I will see you then. Good-bye."

Tricia put the phone back and sat down. She could not believe this; she was in total shock. She had felt an immediate connection with Melanie as well and thought it would be fun to work with her. She didn't expect a call until the following week, and that would have been for a second interview. It finally sank in that she didn't have to wait; she had the job.

Tricia started jumping up and down and hollering. She started dancing with the broom she had propped against the wall and singing about having a job. As she twirled around, she almost ran into Tim and the kids standing at the door, staring at her.

"I got the job!" Tricia sang to them.

"Did you?" Tim asked.

The kids started yelling, and Tim grabbed her and started dancing with her; chaos followed. It took awhile before it quieted down enough for Tim to get the details.

"So, what did she say?" he asked.

Tricia told them all about the interview and the phone call. She told them about the training and how the new company was going to work around her schedule.

"Wow, they must have been impressed with you, Trish, to do that. Good for you. Well, I guess it is root beer floats again. We have been celebrating a lot lately. I am almost sick of root beer floats." Tim laughed.

"Let's have orange then, Daddy. That will make it even more special," Sophie suggested.

"Orange it is. Let's go celebrate. You know life is great when it seems you have celebrated too much lately." They all started to dance and sing around the kitchen as they gathered what they needed to make orange floats.

At dinner, Tricia and Tim discussed scheduling for the weeks ahead. He had a brake job to do this evening and an oil change on Sunday. Another guy wanted him to help his son next Wednesday. She didn't know exactly how her schedule would go until after her meeting on Monday. It would take cooperation and organization to take care of everything.

"You know, Trish, I will just wait until we see how your schedule works out, and I will pick two nights a week when you will be home and I will work then. I can also do small jobs on Sunday afternoons. I won't work on Saturdays at all. That way, we have all of Saturday and Sunday morning as family time. I still want a night with you as well. It will be hard, but we will figure it out."

"Melanie said the new job was a nine-to-five position, so it should be easy enough to get a schedule going. You get off work at three and are home in time for the kids to get off the bus. If you start dinner, we can eat when I get home at 5:30, and then you are free to go. That way it is easier with sharing the car as well. If you have to go to their place to do work, you are going to need a car. I will clean up and help the kids with homework. The three nights you are not working, we will take care of the house. Save Thursdays, like Grammy Ti said, for the big clean-up. I think we could have Saturday night as our time after the kids go to bed," Tricia said, smiling up at Tim. "Would that work for you?"

"That sounds great to me." Tim smiled back. "As long as we get time together, the rest will work out. If I have learned anything, it is that we need to put ourselves first."

"Now that we have that figured out, let's go set up the automatic payments." Tricia hated to get back down to business. It was very good to celebrate something this big. She could not believe that she was starting such an exciting job. A year ago, she would never have dreamed this was possible.

"Let's clean up this mess and then, after we get the kids to bed, we will go to the computer and see what we need to do."

It was late when they finally got to sit down and go into their online banking. They called the toll-free number and got someone to help them. They found it was easy to set up an automatic payment out of their account. One by one, they went through their bills and set them up to be paid the week before they were due. The bank employee suggested they do that because there was a time delay between the date of payment and date received. They did not want to make any more late payments. They had also set up an appointment to go into the bank on Tuesday to open their new savings account. They will be able to do automatic payments into that account as well. They finished in a little more than an hour.

"That was so easy. How could we not know about this?" Tricia asked Tim.

"Where would we learn it, from our parents? They didn't know any of this. We didn't learn it in school. If we didn't have Ti, we would still be in a mess. I haven't found one place online that tells you step-by-step how to do this, but your grandmother knew. That is not right."

"I know. I am so grateful for her. I can't wait to show her that we have done our homework again. It makes me feel so good to take the next step. I feel like I am making headway out of this mess. Everything is automatic now, so it should be pretty hard to screw up. I am exhausted. It has been a long day and I can barely keep my eyes open. Are you ready for bed?"

"Yeah, I will be there in a minute. I just want to check one more time that all the bills are covered. By the way, I am proud of you, Trish." Tim looked at her seriously.

"Thanks," Trish said as she leaned over to kiss him. "I am proud of you too."

Lesson from Chapter 21

A Positive Attitude Goes a Long Way

When many people are suffering, they look for someone who can bring them hope. Many feel that today's beacon of hope is Barack Obama. His "Yes We Can" slogan has inspired Americans, as well as people around the world. His positive message has brought hope during this financial crisis.

We gravitate toward those who look at the brighter side of life, because they make us feel better. We try to avoid anyone who is negative or critical. When searching for a job opportunity in hard times, a positive attitude can set you apart from other candidates. Be positive and grateful, and you will be a step ahead of your competition.

Chapter 22 – The Journey Is More Important than the Destination

On Saturday, everyone was busy trying to get ready for their trip to Ti's. Tricia had sworn the kids to secrecy about her new job. She explained that she wanted to be the one to tell Grammy Ti. The kids looked forward to staying overnight again. They were wondering what surprise their great-grandmother had in store for them this time.

They had not been inside Ti's house for more than a few seconds when Sophie blurted out that her mom had some big news. Tricia looked at her and shook her head. She had hoped Sophie could wait. There was nothing to do but tell the news.

"Well, I had hoped to at least get to sit down before telling you, but I guess you may as well know that I am a full-time employee." Tricia tried hard to keep her emotions in check, but she was struggling not to cry.

"I am so proud of you, girl. I knew someone would recognize what an asset you would be for their company. I am so happy for you." She went over and hugged Tricia.

"I would never have done it without you, Grammy Ti," Tricia replied.

"Oh yes you would. It may have taken a little longer, but eventually you would have figured out that you had to make more money. I just helped you see that you could make more money doing something you like; that's all. Now let's get out of the hallway and into the living room. First, kids, I have a new art project for you. Do you want to see?"

They all followed her to the kitchen table. There were two large white canvases with a series of paint pots filled with vibrant colors. "You two are going to make me some masterpieces to hang in that empty space in the front hall. The only rule is that you have to use your fingers. There are rags there to wipe your hands between colors, so you can make any picture you want. What do you think?"

Both Sophie and Kyle looked skeptical. They weren't allowed to paint with their hands. It seemed odd to agree with Grammy Ti's proposal.

"Don't look so scared. I thought kids liked to get messy. I want you to paint with your hands, because then you can feel the art. That is important if you want to be a good artist. I have smocks here to keep your clothes from getting messy, and when you are all done, we will get you cleaned up so you won't even know your hands touched the paint. Okay?" Ti was a little shocked that they weren't dying to get their hands on the paint.

"Okay, I'll try," said Sophie.

"Me too," said Kyle.

They both got their smocks on and sat down in front of their canvases.

"Well, let's go in the living room and we will talk about your new job and your homework."

Tricia and Tim followed her into the living room. Tricia thought back to the first time she walked in here, just a few months ago. Now, instead of being nervous, it was almost like coming home.

"Well, what is the job and when do you start? I want details," Ti said with a smile.

"Grammy Ti, I am so excited. It is in the purchasing department at Burkhart and Associates."

"Well, well, well, Burkhart and Associates. That is a fine company to work for," Ti said with a touch of pride in her voice.

"You know I felt disappointed I didn't get the other job, but I look at this one and it seems perfect. I am starting in a junior position. That way, I have a chance to learn and get some experience. And if

I work hard, the sky is the limit. Also, the woman I am going to be working for is great. I know I am going to enjoy it. They are going to let me train part time until I can finish with work. I will find out all the details on Monday, but it looks as if I will double my take-home pay. I'll be working nine to five, which is perfect for our family." The more Tricia talked about it, the more excited she became.

"I am so happy for you. All you had to do was keep on trying. That was it. You discovered what you liked and then looked for opportunities in that field. That led you to apply online. If you hadn't, you wouldn't have known your boss was thinking of letting you go. You wouldn't have known there were jobs in an area that excited you, and we would not be celebrating now. That's why people are stuck in life. They just won't take that first step or they start and then stop at the first sign of defeat."

"Grammy, I think people are stuck because of fear. Fear of leaving your comfort zone, even if it isn't that comfortable. Fear of rejection or fear of people thinking you are stupid or unqualified. Remember, I thought no one would hire me because I didn't have any experience. I didn't see myself as worthy, so why would anyone else? I was wrong. I am sure, without Tim's encouragement, I would have quit after the first *no*, because it proved I didn't have what it takes. And you are right about taking that first step. Going online and seeing all of those jobs gave me the confidence to move forward and to apply. I felt that even if no one replied to my applications, I had done something, and that was better than nothing."

"That's the spirit I was looking for, Patricia. That is why you have moved from bleak to hopeful to successful. You took the first steps and kept on moving. Great work, both of you. You now have to look at how this change is going to affect your family."

"We were talking about that last night. We have set up a tentative schedule for the kids and the house, and I think having Trish work full time is not going to be as bad as we originally thought," Tim replied.

"That might have something to do with you stepping up to the plate and taking on some responsibility, Tim. That is the only way this would have worked." Ti looked at Tim and gave him a little nod. "So you have worked out a schedule at home; what about the bills?"

Ti was never one to let the conversation veer from the important for too long.

"With the help of a great Grand National Bank employee, we have everything set up automatically. We are ready to pay down debt and build some savings. It was a lot easier than I thought. What about your adviser? Did you talk to her?" Tim asked Ti.

"Yes, she is going to call your house on Monday and set up an appointment. I told her I had suggested that you interview a couple of advisers, and she was fine with that. It is as important to her as it is to you to find a good match. Did you get any other recommendations?"

"I did get a name from a guy at work. I thought if we start with two and don't find someone we feel comfortable with, then we will keep searching until we do. Do you think that will work?"

"I do; just don't feel any pressure to go with my adviser. She is at the point where she isn't looking for new clients. Susan is doing me a favor. She is great, though." Ti just couldn't help herself. Susan Murphy had been an angel sent from heaven when Ti's husband died. Ti knew nothing about finances other than how to stretch a dollar. She knew she was vulnerable, but Susan had taken her time and helped Ti build a comfortable retirement. Ti owed her a lot, yet it was Susan coming to her rescue again. "Susan will fine tune your plan. She will take care of all your investment needs, as well as let you know what she thinks about your debt repayment plan. She knows everything, so I am sure she will address all the areas I haven't covered."

"I feel confident about our plan, but we don't know anything about investments. Is our emergency money in the right place? Where do we put our money that we want to save long term? How do we make 10 percent?" You could see a little panic sweep across Tim's face.

"Those are all great questions for the two advisers you are interviewing. How they answer that may decide who you will choose. Listen with your ears and your gut. If it sounds too good to be true, it probably is. I know that your emergency money needs to be somewhere safe so the principal is never at risk. Long-term money is a different matter. No one can guarantee 10 percent a year,

Lessons from the Depression

but they can show you investments that have averaged out to 10 percent over the long run. Learn about the pros and cons and then decide, just like you did with the debt plan," Ti explained.

"So we are looking at the emotional versus financial again, eh?" Tim looked at Ti and smiled.

"That's why you have to listen with your gut as well." Ti smiled back. "We dealt with the homework but not lunch. Are you hungry?"

After cleaning up the paints and the kids, everyone sat down to another fine lunch. It was hours before Trisha and Tim were ready to go.

"Now, the kids are fine here, so go out and celebrate on me. While you were having lunch, I went and made reservations at Samola's. I have already paid the bill. It is my gift to you both for being such great students." Ti always had a hard time hiding her pride in her children, and her granddaughter was no different.

"Grammy Ti, you can't do that. That is way too generous. We have pasta at home we can make." Tricia could not believe that her grandmother reserved a table for them.

"Aren't you just dying to go out and have a great meal served to you with a great bottle of wine? Go, enjoy! I have already taken care of everything. I have pre-ordered your meal, so you can't get out of it now. Go home, get dressed up, and have a night on the town on me while I get the wonderful pleasure of spending time with the kids. I think I am getting the better end of the deal, myself," Ti said, looking over at Sophie and Kyle.

"I just don't feel right about this, Ti. This is too much," Tim said, shaking his head.

"What do you think the chances are that you can change my mind?" Ti looked him straight in the eye with her hands on her hips.

"I give. You win. If I have learned anything, it is that you are the master and I am the slave." Tim did a dramatic bow to her.

"That's better. Reservations are for seven, and go there with an empty stomach, because I have some real treats waiting for you. It is my favorite restaurant, and I have arranged for you to try all of my favorite dishes as well as enjoy a great bottle of wine."

"Grammy Ti, that sounds great. We are so grateful. We would have been happy going home tonight, but we haven't had a night out like this in a long time. Thank you so much." Ti went over and hugged her grandmother. She couldn't believe that she would do this for them.

"Well, we better get going so we can prepare to look good for this feast," Tim said, looking at Tricia. "All kidding aside, this is very nice of you." He bent down and gave Ti a hug as well.

Tricia and Tim gave the kids a hug good-bye and headed out to the car. As soon as they were inside the car, Tricia looked at Tim and blurted out, "Do you believe this? I can't believe it. She is sending us to one of the most expensive restaurants in town."

"Relax. It is great that she has done this, but it isn't that big of a deal."

"Are you kidding me? I have wanted to go there for so long, but I knew I would never be able to afford it. Not only is this a great date, it is a dream come true for me. This must have cost her a fortune."

"She seemed pleased with herself, so she must be able to afford it. Let's just enjoy it, Trish. Let's celebrate all the good that has come into our lives, especially your grandmother."

"I am going to enjoy tonight. What am I going to wear? I wasn't prepared to be going out like this." Trisha started mentally going through her closet. She had a couple of outfits in mind, and she was wondering what shoes and purse would go with each.

"We are not going shopping for a new outfit," Tim added, half teasing.

"You know I wouldn't think of it. I was going through in my mind what I could wear from my own collection. So there." Tricia stuck her tongue out at Tim. She knew he had been teasing her, and it felt good. They were much closer than they had been for a while, and Tricia was able to laugh at his good-natured teasing rather than be offended by it.

When they got home, they both spent a considerable amount of time getting ready. They knew this was special and they both wanted to enjoy it. It was 6:30 before they were ready to go.

The restaurant was beautiful; they sat at a private table in a cozy corner in the back. They felt like they were the only ones in the restaurant. Ti had picked out appetizers as well as entrees and desserts. Tim and Tricia couldn't believe the extravagance they were enjoying. They took their time and savored every bite. This was a night neither of them would forget.

On the drive home, they were both quiet. Finally, Tim broke the silence. "What are you thinking about, Trish?"

"I am thinking about how much my life has changed, yet hasn't changed at all. I was trying to figure out what the biggest difference was. I think it would have to be that I now have faith that everything is going to work out, so I can just sit back and enjoy life. I was so consumed with worry and fear about bankruptcy and divorce that I almost made them happen. We are not any richer than we were six months ago, but I feel richer. Isn't that weird?"

"I know what you are saying, Trish. Life looks different now."

"Look at how many days I wasted being upset and worried. If someone had said to me back then that it was going to be okay, I might not have wasted my time being miserable. I was in such a bad place that I probably wouldn't have believed anyone anyway." Tricia never wanted to feel that complete lack of hope again.

"I have watched the guys at work go through this as well, Trish. It's not just us. As soon as they started working on their own financial problems, they changed as well. It is so weird to see. Everyone is happier, and we are sharing budget tips instead of talking about cars. It seems like every day another guy joins the group. Everyone wants to know what drugs we are on. When they first find out we are talking debt and investments, they think we are crazy. But sure enough, they're now doing it too. We have a contest to see who can make the most money on the side. Everyone has different ideas. John has started repairing computers. You know what a nut he is about that. Chris's wife has started an in-home day care. She figures if she is staying home with the kids, she may as well make money. Shawn is now a driver for senior citizens. We love hearing his stories. Some of his clients are lonely and tell him everything, and I mean everything. No one had thought about doing something outside Fairfax. Just like me, they were waiting for overtime to start again. Funny thing is, with this economy, there probably won't be overtime for a while."

"Those guys all went out and found second jobs as well?" Tricia couldn't believe that Tim had the guys at work doing this as well.

"They all had more money going out than in, just like us. They're following Ti's model. They decreased their spending but still needed money. None of them had a hard time coming up with a way to make money. In fact, almost all of them had thought about it but never did anything. They love their second jobs because they are having fun doing something they love. Like me, it is not work."

"Tonight was all about success. I think one of the most important lessons I learned is that there are no quick fixes in life. Success is a long journey. To fix this mess, it will take us ten years, and that is just fine with me now. In the beginning, I did want a one-day solution. I would have taken that check from Grammy Ti or loved a lottery win or whatever. Now I know that if I had taken the quick fix, I would have missed the other wonderful changes that have happened in our lives. I almost believe that our money problems were just a reflection of all the other problems going on in our lives. Let's face it—we were not living life before. Neither one of us was very happy. We were just surviving. Now I feel more alive than ever. I am enjoying every moment. It is fine that it will take years for us to be rich. I am going to enjoy every minute making it happen with you, Sophie, and Kyle. I don't need to shop anymore. I enjoyed tonight at the restaurant, but I also enjoyed our night of Hamburger Helper," Trisha confessed.

"I feel the same way, Trish. It is not about things. It is about people now, and the time I spend with you and the kids is my joy. Well, that and working on cars," Tim said, laughing. "Some of the guys have been selling all the stuff they thought they needed but didn't. One of them said that selling his boat was like a big weight off his shoulders. He knew he couldn't afford it, but he thought he needed it to make him and his family happy. Turns out that his wife and kids hated boating. They started playing this crazy card game instead and they love it. He said they rarely talked when they were on the boat. Each of them would be in their separate corners. Through playing cards, he feels closer to his kids. They talk about everything. He wondered why he couldn't see this before. It is so simple. You are right, Trish. Everything we have done is simple common sense. Why couldn't we figure it out?"

"I wonder if it is because when you are in the middle of everything, you just can't think straight." Trish was amazed at how far they had come. She knew they both could see clearly now.

"I am not sure about that. I am happy that we are on the right path now. Thanks to Ti, we should be back on track in a few years. A few simple steps and we will be fine. Who knew? I can't wait to meet with an expert to make this plan a reality. Until then, I think I will just enjoy having my wife all to myself." Tim knew that of all the things that had happened over the last few months, tonight had been the best.

Lessons from Chapter 22

Don't Let Fear Stop You

The number-one cause of inaction is fear. You fear that if you did anything, it would make it worse. You may fear humiliation or you may just fear failure.

To be successful, you need to conquer worry and fear. This will probably be your most difficult task. Believe that the universe is conspiring on your behalf. Believe that you cannot make a wrong move. Make a pledge to yourself that you will not let fear stop you or dictate your decisions.

Success Is a Long Journey

It will only be in hindsight that you will realize that everything you have gone through has been to make your life better. A successful life is a long journey filled with both wonderful and dreadful moments. In the midst of misery, it is difficult to see how it can help you in the long run. But if you rise above it and move forward, one day you will have the clarity of hindsight to know that every step on your journey to success was the right one, painful or not.

Chapter 23 – Investments 101

On Monday, Susan called as promised and made an appointment for the following night. It was hectic Monday and Tuesday for Tricia, trying to coordinate two different jobs. Her boss had agreed to only one week of notice, so she would only have to do the juggling act for a few more days. She felt excited to meet Susan, to find out what they needed to get a real financial plan in place.

"We have dealt with the debt and income part, so now I am ready for the investment planning. I want to get that savings program going, and we haven't even talked about life and disability insurance. We will have to have that discussion as well. I want to make sure that we have everything taken care of, no matter what life hands us," Tricia told Susan.

"Well, Tricia and Tim, you have done a great job on the income and expenses. I think I may have to hire Ti on as part of my team. When we are dealing with investments, there are a few steps we have to take before we choose the investment itself. The first step is to find out what your financial goals are. I have to know where you want to go before I can tell you how to get there."

Susan had them fill out several questionnaires that outlined different areas of their financial picture. After answering the questions and having a lengthy discussion, Tim and Tricia had identified four clear goals: They wanted the emergency fund set up and funded. They wanted another savings account for short- and medium-term purchases and expenses. They also wanted investment accounts for the kids' educations and their retirement. They ranked them in that order of importance.

"Now that we determined your goals, I need to know what type of investor you are. Everyone is different. I have several questions to pinpoint your risk tolerance and timeline. We want to make sure that your investments satisfy both your financial and emotional needs." Susan pulled out the second set of questions.

"Where have we heard that before?" Tim asked Tricia with a wink. "We have never discussed investments before, so I have no idea what type of investor I am."

"When you answer all of these questions, you will know," Susan told Tim. "Some of your answers may surprise you, and you will be shocked that the two of you can answer them so differently. Often one partner is conservative and the other is a gambler. Let's see who's who."

It took awhile to get through all the questions. Some answers were surprising. Tim was more conservative than Tricia. They had both thought it would have been the other way around.

"Based on your answers and timeframe, I would have four different accounts set up. You would have your emergency account at the bank. That account is great because you have access if an emergency comes up, but you can't access it at a point of sale. You can't just go out and buy a pair of shoes with it. You know how men are with their shoes, Tricia." Susan couldn't help but laugh. She knew enough to know that Tim could take a joke. "The other benefit of the account is that the principal is safe. You will not get much interest, but you know the money you put in will still be there when you need it. So we have met goal number one."

"What do you mean 'the principal is safe'? Does that mean it is safe enough to buy shoes?" Tim shot back. "Seriously, when is the money safe and when isn't it?"

"Well, for some investments, the value may go up or down based on the underlying market that it is in. For instance, a stock in a company is valued by the amount the last person who bought it was willing to pay. That number may be higher or lower than you paid for it. When you sell your investment, you will get whatever the buyer will pay then. Most stocks increase in value over time, so they are an investment you would use for money you didn't need for the next ten or twenty years."

"Like our retirement?" Tricia asked.

"Yes, that would be a consideration for your retirement account. But not for money you may need soon. If your stock goes down, your emergency account would be worth less than $500, and that would defeat the purpose. So we go safe and accessible in a bank account," Susan replied.

"For your medium-term savings, we have a couple of choices. Because you are investing a small amount monthly, the best bet is a mutual fund with a higher yield than a bank account, but a lower risk than a stock."

"What is a mutual fund?" Tim asked.

"A mutual fund is a way for small investors to pool their money together so they can own a more diversified group of investments with little money. A fee is paid out of the pool of money to a manager, who buys and sells the underlying investments. There are three advantages to this: One, you have an expert choosing the investments for you. Two, you could have twenty to over a hundred investments in your portfolio. This lessens your risk. If one investment is not doing well and that is all you owned, you would be on the losing end of the equation. If you had twenty investments and only one was performing poorly, you are still making money. Ever hear of the expression 'all your eggs in one basket'? That means if you had all of your eggs in one basket and the handle broke and the eggs tumbled out, you would have a horrible gooey mess on your hands. But if you had two baskets and the handle broke on one of them, half of your eggs are still safe. Make sense?" Susan looked over a Tim and Tricia to see if they were following.

"It does make sense to me, I guess. But I have never heard that expression explained like that before," Tricia replied.

Susan started to laugh. "That is from personal experience, I am afraid. That was my job growing up, getting the eggs every morning. Believe me, when the handle breaks, it is a gooey mess. My mom taught me to split them between two baskets, and it is a great way for me to picture diversification."

"We don't want a gooey mess, so we put our trust in you to make sure we are diversified," Tim said.

"So you now understand the idea of diversification. The third advantage of an open mutual fund is that it is fairly liquid. That means when you need the money, you can get your hands on it within three to five business days. This gives you the flexibility to access your investments and to make changes if needed. That is important, because unexpected needs will come up and your goals will change over the next ten years, so you have to have some flexibility."

"So, we just buy a mutual fund and we are good to go for our second savings account?" Tricia asked.

"The simple answer is yes. But you need to understand that 'mutual fund' is a generic term. It is a way to invest, rather than an investment. There are different categories of mutual funds, based on what they invest in. So we need to find the right investment first and then buy a mutual fund that holds that investment. Because your timeframe is less than five years for this money, we do not want to even consider buying a stock. That is because there is a risk that it would be worth less in five years. So we have to look at something that will hold its value. Because you want to add to your investment every month, you have two choices. You can use short-term treasury bills put out by the government or short-term bonds. T-bills usually hold their value and pay out interest over a short period of time like sixty or ninety days. The interest rate is not high, but it is better than most bank accounts. Bonds have a longer term to them, so they often pay a higher annual yield. The longer the term, the better the interest rate, but over that period of time, the value of the underlying bond can change, because it's affected when interest rates go up or down. So a money market fund that holds T-bills or a short-term bond fund would be a good choice for you. The general rule of thumb is the more risk you take, the higher the possible return. Bonds usually average a higher return than T-bills because there is more market risk. That is a condensed version of how T-bills and short-term bonds work, but do you get the general idea?" Susan wanted to make sure she wasn't confusing them even more.

"I think so. We just want to make sure we are not taking a huge risk with this money, because we may need it in a few years. So we are taking a smaller risk of it changing in value to make a higher return than a bank account, but not as much as the stock market. So if we were to buy a short-term bond fund, is it possible we would be down in two years?" Tricia felt like she was getting it, but she wanted to make sure.

"There is a risk of that. Bonds lose value when interest rates go up. But they return to their original value when they mature. If we stick to short-term bonds that are closer to their due date, there is less price volatility and therefore less risk of a lower value. There are no guarantees, though. We would choose the bonds over the T-bills because of the better rate of return overall," Susan replied.

"I don't like the sound of risk in that account, Susan. I would rather deal with a T-bill that holds its value. We don't know when we may need the money, so I want it safe. We could look at bonds for some of the longer-term investments." Tim looked over at Tricia. "What do you think?"

"I would like to make more interest, and I know the odds are in our favor to do that, but I am worried too. I say T-bill as well. Do you think that is wise, Susan?"

"Financially it would probably work out better in the bond fund, but I can see your concern, and emotion always trumps financial. We will set up the money market fund and get you contributing into it from your bank account every month. In a few years, if you have built up some cash, we could possibly move part of it over to a bond fund so you have both. Sound good?" Tricia and Tim nodded. "Then let's talk about the education account. Kyle will be going to school in about ten years, right?"

"That's right," Tricia answered. "It is hard to believe."

"This gives us a longer time horizon so we can talk about stocks. If you invest in a mutual fund that holds stocks, it is valued at the end of every day of trading. They add up the value of all the underlying stocks and divide by the number of outstanding units. If each unit's value was $10 and you owned ten units, your investment would be worth $100. You can have a portfolio that has one type of stock, like only large companies. You can have a portfolio of investments of one country, such as a U.S. stock fund, or you can have various stocks that invest in several countries. Not all stocks are alike. You increase your risk when you buy smaller, unproven companies. You also increase your risk if you buy a mutual fund that holds stocks in one category like precious metals or oil and gas. You also have a currency risk when you invest outside your country, because the portfolio has to be converted back to your dollar. The longer you have before you need the money, the more risk you can afford financially. But you have to be able to handle that risk emotionally as well."

"This sounds complicated. I get the different risks, but how do we know what to choose?" Tim asked.

"That is why I had you do the risk-profile questionnaire. I have learned what your thoughts are about market conditions before I make any recommendations. I now know that you are not a big gambler and you like a safer bet. Tricia wants the best return with the lowest amount of risk. Therefore, I would never put either of you in an aggressive fund. We will look at where there is a moderate amount of risk that we will try to reduce as much as possible through diversification. I am thinking a balanced fund that holds both stocks and bonds is the best bet for your kids' education fund. It will give you a decent rate of return with diversification that reduces the investment risk in the portfolio. Does that sound like the investment you were looking for?" Susan was hoping she was not talking over their heads. There was no easy way to explain all of this, but it was important to her to educate her clients so they could make informed choices.

"I think you have it right, Susan. We don't want to take a huge risk, but we do want to make around 10 percent. Do you think it is possible with the balanced fund?" Tricia wanted to make sure that Susan was aware of their target return.

"That is the high end for a balanced fund. Your expectation should be in the 5 to 7 percent range, but there have been periods where some balanced funds have had higher returns than that; 10 percent is more probable in a stock mutual fund. But again, we can only look at what these funds have done in the past. There are no guarantees for the future." Susan felt it was important that they understood that. Many investors had been disappointed in the past because of unrealistic expectations.

"I think the balanced fund is the right choice for the kids. I would like to talk about stocks for our retirement, though. We have more time because we won't need that money for thirty years. I think that we might as well take advantage of that. Would you feel comfortable with that, Tim?" Tricia wanted to make sure that they were both on the same page.

"I think so. I don't get all of this, but I think we have to go by risk. So we pick the risk based on timeframe, and that means no risk for the emergency fund, little risk for the savings, a medium amount of risk for the kids, and the most risk for our retirement. I feel like I am reciting the story of the Three Bears." He started to laugh.

"It is just like that story, Tim. We are matching personality and preference with the right investment. I just might steal that analogy for other clients."

"I expect some royalties on that, Susan," Tim said with a wink.

"All kidding aside, that is how it is done. Once we know the category of investment, I use my expertise to pick the right mutual fund. I am up to date on all the fund managers and portfolios, so I can choose a fund that is right for you. That is how the process works. Do you have any questions?"

"My head hurts. I think I learned more about investing in the last two hours than I have in the last twenty years. I can say that I trust you. I feel that I have learned enough to at least know what the risks are. I am not going into this blind," Tim said, rubbing his temples.

"I feel the same way, Susan. Thanks for educating us. I feel more confident in deciding what is right for us," Tricia added. "We are meeting with another adviser tomorrow, so would it be okay if we get back to you at the end of the week? I enjoyed sitting down with you, and I can't see how anyone could compete with you."

"I have had years of experience, Tricia. Sometimes that makes all the difference. The more clients you meet, the more analogies you gain to explain this complicated business just a little bit better."

She smiled at Tim. "Whatever your decision, I enjoyed meeting you both."

Susan put all the papers into Tim and Tricia's file and packed up her briefcase. After she left, Tim and Tricia went over their notes.

"I liked her," Tricia said.

"Me too," Tim agreed. "Can't wait to see what this other guy has to say. That is a hard act to follow."

Lessons from Chapter 23

Clear Financial Goals

Your financial goals need to be clear to create a plan to reach them. They should be specific in dollar amount and timeframe. Each goal should be considered individually so your risk tolerance for each is established and a suitable investment account created. You should only deal with a financial adviser who will take the time to go through the lengthy interview needed to determine these individual goals as part of an overall financial plan. The adviser should also have the proper credentials and experience to ensure you get the best advice possible.

Mutual Funds

"Mutual fund" is a generic term to describe how assets are pooled together and invested. The type varies drastically, depending on the underlying investment. If you hear someone say they will never invest in a mutual fund again because they lost money, they have been in the wrong type for their particular goal. The advantages of a mutual fund are professional management, diversification, and liquidity, without needing a large initial investment.

Chapter 24 – Sometimes Old-Fashioned Is Best

Tricia and Tim's meeting on Wednesday night was not as enjoyable as their appointment with Susan. David Marks had as much experience and knew as much, but he didn't explain everything the way Susan did. Neither Tim nor Tricia felt as comfortable as they did the previous night. It was an easy choice for them to ask Susan to be their financial adviser.

The week flew by as Tricia balanced her two jobs and Tim did a couple of oil changes for his friends. They were both exhausted by Friday but felt good about their accomplishments. Again, the highlight of their week was the trip to Ti's.

By this time, going to Ti's was like putting on an old sweater. It felt warm and cozy and comfortable. Tricia had wondered aloud in the car if anyone even remembered life before Grammy Ti. Kyle was funny when he said he didn't ever want to remember that life again. He only wanted a "Grammy Ti life."

When they got inside, Ti had the craft table ready and coffee waiting in the living room. It was easy and comfortable for her as well.

"Well, how was your week?" she asked.

"It was great, Grammy Ti," Tricia replied. "We met both of the advisers, and Susan won hands down. Now we know why you like her so much. We are going to meet with her on Monday again to set up all the accounts. I have my salary worked out for my new job, so we redid the budget and have come up with figures for all the accounts. We think we can have the $500 in the emergency account in just one month. Isn't that great?"

"And we had a great time last weekend. That restaurant was amazing. Thank you so much," Tim added.

"Oh yeah, Grammy Ti, outside of your homemade soup, that was the best meal I have ever tasted."

"You are both welcome, but I think Samola's has better food than my soup. Thank for buttering me up, though," Ti replied with a smile. "So you have done your budget, increased your incomes, set up your savings and investments. I guess my work here is done."

"Oh, I don't think so, Grammy Ti. You are like our money coach. We have to come here every week and check our stats and see where we need to improve. Right, Tim?"

"We need someone to keep us on the straight and narrow. We may just have to make it twice a week." Tim smiled. "All kidding aside, we need to keep visiting you because you make the best lunch." At this point Tim couldn't keep from laughing.

"Grammy Ti, lunch is the best here, but I would like to keep this schedule if it is fine with you. I enjoy visiting you and I think sometimes the kids would rather live here than at home. We are going to need help when we hit bumps and roadblocks. Would you mind if we come here every Saturday? I know you do have a life and we just barged in on it," Tricia said apologetically.

"I would love to have you keep coming. It is the best part of my week." Ti was having a hard time keeping her emotions in check.

"We would also like you to come for dinner every Wednesday." Tricia was hoping this wouldn't be too much for her grandmother.

"Are you sure? You are both busy. I don't want you to feel like you have to."

"Have to? You're the best part of our week too, Ti. We had so much fun the last time you came over. And now that our life is a celebration every day, we are happy to have you join in. You made it happen." Tim sincerely believed that.

"Well, it would be an honor then."

Ti was as happy as she had ever been. It was like the old days when her son Kyle would bring Patricia over when she was small. Excitement and laughter were back in her life and she was grateful. They all enjoyed the rest of the afternoon and left with the promise of seeing one another Wednesday.

Tricia and Tim had a hard time getting the kids settled down to bed that night, so it was late when they finally got to sit down and talk.

"You know, Trish, I think we have made some big steps toward being able to handle what life dishes out. Look what we have already done. And when we meet with Susan this week, we will talk about insurance and anything else we may not have thought about before. We will deal with it the same way we have dealt with everything else. We will look at the pros and cons and then decide what is important to us. Then and only then will we incorporate it into our financial plan. At some point, we will have dealt with everything, and then we can let the plan take care of itself. So there is nothing left to worry about."

"Look at us, Tim, two young people living life the old-fashioned way. Instead of going for the quick fix, we are taking care of everything the hard, 'taking responsibility for our actions' way. It's a big change for us."

"Look at how many times we tried the quick fix and it made it worse and cost us money. But it always seemed too hard to do it the long way. We were talking about it at work. Shane brought in a video he bought from a late-night TV ad. You know those infomercials. It promised to clear up your debt in seven days. We were all excited to watch it. This was back when I was still in the 'give me something easy' mode. We laughed through the whole video. First, it was cheesy. Second, it gave the wrong information. Some of the Web sites listed weren't even up and running. It was the biggest waste of money. It said that you could pay only half of your debt and not hurt your credit rating. Of course, you could do this after paying a whopping fee. We called a credit counseling service and asked if that was possible, and we got a different answer. They said if you negotiate with a credit card company and pay off less than the balance, it would hurt your credit score. It would be better than bankruptcy, but it would still have an effect. In fact, the woman we spoke to thought the way we were doing it was the best way to protect our credit score. Negotiating debt should only come when there is no other way but bankruptcy. If that happens, there are legitimate counseling firms that will help you. Shane spent over two hundred dollars on that video. What a waste. But you buy it because you want it to be easy."

"How come you never told me about this before? We should have borrowed it and watched it together." Tricia was a little upset that there may have been another way.

"Didn't you hear me, Trish? It was crap. The way Ti taught us is the only way. We can do this. Shane may have to go into bankruptcy because he has done everything but he is still in over his head. That is why he bought the DVD. He was desperate. Remember what Ti said: if you have done everything you can and still can't balance your budget, then you go see a professional. We don't need to do that. This way it will be hard in the next couple of years, but we will have clean credit and be out of this mess. You should see how upset Shane is over this. It has almost destroyed him, because he doesn't want to declare bankruptcy. He got caught up in some balloon payment for his mortgage and he can't keep up. The house is worth less than the mortgage, and he has nothing else. He is fighting for his life right now. We have all been trying to help him, but it almost makes it worse because we have balanced our budgets and he hasn't. He is now trying to negotiate with the mortgage company. We are all praying for him." Tim looked over at Trish. He felt so lucky to be where they were. He knew that if they hadn't listened to Ti, it could have been them.

"That is awful, Tim. I can't believe it. I was jealous because their house was so much bigger. I thought they had it made. I have learned so much over the past few months, and if you have been passing that information along to Shane, he may have a chance. He has lowered his expenses, increased his income, and he is now negotiating to make the payments better. If I have learned anything, it is that you never know how it will work out. I could never have dreamed this would happen for us. I did not know any of this was possible, so Shane might be able to work it out too. I think doing something, anything, makes it better."

"Okay, Ti," Tim said with a smirk. "We keep encouraging him, and everyone is researching information to help him deal with the bank. He also has an appointment with Credit Counselors Anonymous. He is going to do whatever it takes to make this work. I think with that attitude, he might be able to do it."

"You know, for a minute there, I was a bit ticked off there was a DVD that I didn't get to see that may have made it easier. Now I am glad that we have the opportunity to fix our finances the right way, even if it takes a long time. I am going to be old-fashioned for the rest of my life."

"Does that mean you do all the housework?" Tim teased.

Tricia punched him in the arm. "Old-fashioned in finances only," she said.

"Ouch." Tim feigned pain. "I can see that. I am happy to join you on that long journey, my lady." Tim took his ball cap off and did a sweeping bow in front of Tricia. "I can take the slow ride with you because I know we will live happily ever after." They both began to laugh.

Lessons from Chapter 24

There Is no Easy Way Out

It is human nature that when we get into trouble, we want to get out of it the easiest, least painful way. When you are in debt, there is no easy way. You must either slash your expenses and forgo some of your favorite luxuries or declare bankruptcy, which can haunt you for a long time. Make sure when you are making your plan that you consider all the ramifications. Avoiding pain today could increase it tomorrow. Try everything before resorting to negotiating out of your debt. Then at least you have the peace of mind that you did everything you could. That is all anyone can ask for.

Slow and Steady

Being in debt can be stressful, and it is difficult not to be discouraged looking into the future. You need to concentrate on today. Do what is necessary to make it through on your budget today. Don't even consider "what ifs." Each day is a victory. Celebrate it.

You Can Do It!

If there is one lesson I hope you learn from this story, it is that you can do it. You can change your circumstances and you can change your life. Lack of money is often just a symptom of a life on the wrong course. If you fix your life, then money, happiness, and success will follow. Walk fearlessly into the future with the strong belief that everything will work out. All you have to do is believe!

About the Author

Darlene Gudrie Butts has enjoyed a career as an advisor, author, speaker, and educator in the financial industry for the past 23 years. Her goal has always been to educate and guide her clients so they could reach their financial goals. With the recent credit crunch and the record amount of personal debt acrrued in North America, she decided that it was time to layout a simple strategy to get back on track in an simple and entertaining fashion. Darlene has shown thousands of people that going back to the basics can put you on the path to financial security. She currently resides in Kingsville, Ontario with her husband and three children.

For more information or to book a speaking engagement she may be reached by email at:

lessonsfromthedepression@gmail.com

Take Lessons From The Depression To The Next Level At Lessonsfromthedepression.Net.

Step 1 Go to our website at www.lessonsfromthedepression.net. There you can find a community of people who are also trying to eliminate debt. You can register for free downloads as well as a coupon to reduce the price of the upcoming Lessons from the Depression workbook.

Step 2 Register for the latest teleseminar or look up the Lessons' "Tip of the Week".

Step 3 Download interactive spreadsheets to determine where you are now and get you headed in the direction of where you want to be.

How to Reach Us

Go to lessonsfromthedepression.net or e-mail us at lessonsfromthedepression@gmail.com. We want to hear about your successes and what lessons you have learned as well as any questions that were not answered for you in the book. We will be sharing these with everyone so we can succeed in the money game together!

Printed in the United States
152052LV00012BA/126/P